MW01615618

Spiritual Healing

Spiritual Healing

by Dr. Minamu

Veronica Lane Books
www.veronicalanebooks.com
2554 Lincoln Blvd. Ste 142, Los Angeles, CA 90291 USA
Tel/Fax: +1 (800) 651-1001 / Intl: +1 (310) 745-0162

Library of Congress Cataloging-In-Publication Data
The Library of Congress No. 2011914063
86p. cm

Summary: A medical doctor's guide for lay persons to non-invasive,
complementary and intuitive healing modalities.

Prologue

A Method of Healing Adopted by Jesus Christ

A healing method called "Spiritual Healing" has brought about many verified miracles all around the world, such as curing fatal diseases and reviving the soul. It has delivered hope and pride to many people. It has surely been playing an important role in saving the world.

"Spiritual Healing" is literally a method of healing the human spirit. It has been adopted not only in Japan but also widely overseas since the earliest of times.

For example, many of the miracles that Jesus Christ showed to people of his time were a result of spiritual healing. We can see in written documents that there were many cases in which people recovered from illnesses, such as blind people regaining their sight or people with fatal diseases recovering their strength.

It is often explained that Jesus, who is said to be the son of God, used divine power to achieve these phenomena. However, I must say that the "Principle of Spiritual Healing" explained in Chapter 3 basically brings about almost the same effect.

As for Jesus, he made those miracles happen by harnessing a high-dimensional energy often called the 'Creator', or so to say *qi*.

Jesus was able to realize these unbelievable acts with ease since he was born with a soul of high energy. However, we can see that even today there are many spiritual healers that are active and effective, and making full use of their own discoveries.

The Principle of Healing: *Free your spirit!*

In Chapter 1, I introduce some of the many spiritual healing methods found around the world.

By following my heart I have discovered a unique method of spiritual healing. Working as a doctor, and having been given chances to encounter miraculous synchronicity in daily life, I realized that I had a special talent for healing people. I am proud that I can contribute to people's well being by making use of this talent. In Chapter 4, I pick up and introduce some practical examples of what I have accomplished so that you can become more familiar with spiritual healing.

Through my experience of seeing many clients who have been seized with illnesses such as depression, backache, cancer, hemorrhoids, and so on, but have somehow dramatically recovered, I noticed that these people have more or less experienced an awakening of the soul.

This is actually the essential objective of healing. The mechanism of healing and the method of experiencing an awakening can be explained by the same key phrase: it is to "free your soul."

The impossible becomes possible if you learn to be able to free your soul, and miracles can actually happen around you. Your life may change positively, and your dreams may come true.

If you can free your soul, you will be able to heal yourself and accomplish what you have in mind.

As you may have noticed, the key to succeeding in life and the principle of healing both follow the same philosophy.

How can spiritual healing and succeeding in life both be realized by freeing your soul? Is there a certain way to achieve true freedom? The answers to these questions are carefully discussed in Chapter 3.

So-called "power spots" are also good places to rejuvenate yourself. How can people rejuvenate themselves specifically in power spots? The answer to this question is revealed in Chapter 5. In addition, hints on how to make spaces in your daily life change into power spots are also explained.

Why Healing is Required Today

As you can see, spiritual healing has to do with a broad range of aspects in one's life. It not only cures mental and physical illnesses but goes farther and also heals the soul, supporting the connection between human beings and high-dimensional energy.

In a time when intractable and puzzling diseases, attributed to stress, chemical substances and electromagnetic waves, often attack people, we need these kinds of spiritual healing methods. Furthermore, as karma from the past is revisiting us today, spiritual healing methods are becoming truly indispensable.

Many people will soon realize that spiritual healing is becoming more and more necessary and important as time goes by. As I describe in Chapter 6, we are entering an era in which people can connect with high-dimensional energies with ease. Consequently, it is also becoming easier to connect with low-dimensional energy. Thus the role of spiritual healing in society will become more and more significant.

Spiritual healing works not only for people who are ill, but for practically everybody. There are no restrictions on race, blood type, sex, wealth, or age. It can lead to you attaining the best condition of your life.

It is fair to say that it is the first time in history that people have been given abundant chances to be healed in such way.

I sincerely hope that you will gain a better understanding of what spiritual healing is, and incorporate it into your life. By doing so, individuals will be able to improve their health conditions and reinvigorate their souls, which will lead to a more peaceful, creative, and more highly developed society.

I am certain that if you read through this book, you will become more familiar with spiritual issues, which may have been kept mysteriously veiled otherwise. I hope what is written here can be of help in establishing a better future in your life.

Chapter 1
What is Spiritual Healing?

A Healing Method Approved by Medical Organizations

During my 25 years as a doctor I have seen many patients. One of the most important facts that I discovered during this period is that modern medical treatments cannot solve everything. There is a growing necessity to develop new alternatives. I am confident in the exceptionally high potential of spiritual healing and am certain that it can play a significant role in helping our society face the challenges of today.

Although "spiritual healing" may not be widely recognized in Japan, it is accepted by many medical organizations in Europe and the U.S. as an alternative medical service for healing illnesses or for helping maintain a healthy mind and body.

I have long been providing spiritual healing services in conjunction with my work as a doctor. During this time, I have received favorable feedback from my patients and witnessed cases in which clients recovered to an extent that could not have been expected if only standard medical practices were used. It was these success stories that led me to rediscover the importance of spiritual healing. Spiritual healing is not only used to cure mental and physical illnesses but can also be beneficial in realizing an individual's talent potential, inspiring spiritual growth and overcoming many of the concerns or problems of everyday life.

It was a fortunate coincidence that I was given the chance to read a book written by Harry Edwards (1893-1976), who I respect a great deal, when I began using my unique spiritual healing methods. At that time I was a forerunner in the world of spiritual healing, an area which did not even exist in the medical field in Japan. I felt reassured and encouraged to know that a pioneer like Mr. Edwards had been successful in the same field. I took heart by the fact that my personal experiences were echoed in Mr. Edward's book. Mr. Edwards is an indispensable figure when it comes to spiritual healing, and he is also an important senior healer, one who I truly respect.

Mr. Edwards, who was born in London, is known as a pioneer who introduced spiritual healing to the world. During his time as an army captain and printing company employee he acquired a special talent for spiritual healing and was able to cure many people of their illnesses. His accomplishments were soon recognized and led to a worldwide boom.

As is often the case when new methods are first adopted, Mr. Edwards received criticism for adopting such spiritual methods. However, he did not give in and continued curing people who were in need. Such behavior displayed his dedication and commitment to spiritual healing, and shows why he is so widely respected by many other professionals in the field.

The Royal Family Acknowledges Spiritual Healing

I must say that the numerous accomplishments of Mr. Edwards should be honored. Among the various people who sought Mr. Edward's spiritual treatment are members of the British royal family, judges, ministers, political party leaders, commander-in-chiefs of military forces, musicians and other artists, Olympic athletes, BBC commentators, Christian priests, archbishops and many doctors.

Princess Marie Louise was one of Harry Edwards' many high profile visitors. It can be implied that her interest in spiritual healing indicates that members of the British royal family also acknowledged this method of healing. The princess was physically weak due to her age and is said to have been treated by Mr. Edwards before she took part in Queen Elizabeth's coronation. Mr. Edwards wrote in his book that he was sure that the royal family acknowledged spiritual healing, as he was also invited to the princess' funeral.

Mr. Edwards's spiritual healing treatment is often called the "hand-healing method." He held his hand against the client or actually held the hand of the patient in order to remove the illnesses in the body and soul. Alternately, he used a method called "remote healing," which is done by praying for the patient from a distance. Mr. Edwards seemed to adopt this method most of the time.

Mr. Edwards explained the so-called "hand-healing method" by dividing it into two parts: "magnetic therapy" and "direct therapy." In magnetic therapy, the healer absorbs cosmic energy into his body and pours it into the patient's in turn. In direct therapy, the healer utilizes the healing power of spirits.

Remote healing is a method that enables healers to help those who are living far away and who they haven't personally met. In this case, the patient can be cured even if the healer does not inform the patient when the treatment is actually provided.

No Limits to the Types of Illnesses That Can Be Healed

Direct therapy and remote healing both resemble the methods I favor. What is important to note about these methods of spiritual healing are that they make use of subtle energy that even modern science cannot detect. In oriental medicine this energy is called *'qi'*. Although I will explain more about qi later on, I must mention here that the utilization of qi has long been understood and utilized throughout history.

Mr. Edwards cured various types of illnesses by adopting the spiritual healing methods mentioned above. As is written in his book, "There is no limit in types of illness that can be cured by spiritual healing (although it is restricted within a range defined by the law)." The spiritual healing adopted by Mr. Edwards works swiftly for neuroses, mental disorders, cancers, tuberculosis, and other ailments. It has also been reported that this form of medicine could cure diseases in or improve the condition of internal organs, all types of tumors, paralysis, structural deformities, bone fractures, burn wounds, varicosity, ulcers, lesions or decline in the function of the sensory organs. The fact that five to six thousand patients from both Britain and abroad visit the Harry Edwards Healing Sanctuary every year shows that people are looking for more effective treatments than those offered in general medical facilities. Furthermore, over 80% of patients treated at the sanctuary have been successfully healed.

There were cases in which Mr. Edwards himself thought it was impossible to effect a cure, but due to his belief in his methods he was surprisingly successful in curing his afflicted patients. Mr. Edwards was once called to cure the failing eyesight of a cleric of the Methodist Church. The cleric had lost vision in his left eye 30 years previously and was beginning to lose sight in his right eye. Mr. Edwards focused on healing the right eye without paying particular attention to the left eye. However, both eyes miraculously regained their sight. When another young patient suffering from a disease that had bent his spine into the shape of a 's' came to see him, Mr. Edwards was able to straighten it.

A Method Adopted in Hospitals and Clinics

Following his miraculous healing of patients, as mentioned in the previous two cases, Mr. Edwards became more prominent and was even thought by some to be the second coming of Jesus Christ.

However, Mr. Edwards's achievements should not be recognized merely because he miraculously healed people, but also because he forged a path for the healers that wished to follow him and use his methods.

Following the proposal of Mr. Edwards, the "National Federation of Spiritual Healers" was established in the early 1950s in England. A beneficial association that connects doctors and healers named the "Doctor-Healer Network of England" was also founded. Due to the establishment of these two organizations, the "hand-healing method" came to be acknowledged as an alternative treatment, which allowed many people to benefit from this new healing technique. Spiritual healing began to be adopted in hospitals and clinics in England, and the treatment was soon covered by insurance. Due to this breakthrough the healers that followed could continue their work proactively and positively, saving many people who were in need.

Spiritual healing certainly is a mysterious field that modern science cannot completely explain. It is a concept that those with a critical mind are quick to dismiss. However, if we are to admit that Mr. Edwards has actually helped to cure people's diseases, we must also admit that it is necessary to verify these cases scientifically. I believe that Mr. Edwards has showed us a goal to pursue, thus urging us all to move forward in the same direction. Every day I do the best I can to pursue this goal.

Possibilities of Alternative Therapies

Here I would like to verify the position of spiritual healing from an alternative therapy point of view.

Alternative therapy is not yet widespread in Japan. However, many of the people who go to medical facilities in the U.S. request some form of alternative therapy. The National Comprehensive Cancer Network (NCCM) was established within the National Institutes of Health (NIH) in 1992, the result of the increasing interest of the people. The research conducted there has continued year after year.

Alternative therapy is not a treatment or health management method formally defined in modern medicine. It covers a broad range of solutions such as traditional medicine, folk medicine, supplements, herb therapy, aroma therapy, Chinese medicine (herbal treatment, acupuncture and moxibustion, Shiatsu, and Qigong therapy), alimentotherapy, immune therapy, psychological therapy, hot-spring therapy, oxygen therapy, healing, osteopathy, homeopathy, flower essence therapy, and so on. There is another term used to describe the same thing: "supplementary medicine." This term highlights the fact that alternative therapy is primarily utilized to supplement the efforts of modern medicine. Medicine that integrates modern medicine and alternative therapy is also known as "integrated medicine."

The Worldwide Prominence of Japanese Spiritual Healing

Spiritual healing is introduced as one type of treatment within the field of "hand-healing method" in Keiichi Ueno's book "Introduction to Supplementary Alternative Therapy."

In this book, Mr. Ueno discusses *'johrei'* (to purify spirits) and the therapeutic touch. The former was developed in Japan, and the latter was invented by Dolores Krieger, a professor at New York University.

Despite the difference in category, the methods are similar in that the healer holds their hand against the patient in order to cure any illnesses of the body and soul.

Although we do have some types of hand-healing methods in Japan, such as *'johrei'*, it is not widely accepted due to its religious background. But even if it was not connected with religion, many people might tend to view it with suspicion. In England however, the hand-healing method has been well-accepted and acknowledged as a therapy known as "spiritual healing." I have already explained that this process had a great deal to do with the contributions of Mr. Edwards.

Japanese philosopher and theologian National Federation of Spiritual Healers Katsumi Takizawa talked about his own experiences with *'johrei'* in his book "Modern Medicine and Religion." While suffering from "age-related macular degeneration" and in danger of losing his sight, he was introduced to *'johrei'* by his friend. As a result, he recovered his sight. He was not only able to see without having any sense of discomfort, but the feeling in other parts of his body also improved. *'Johrei'* is a method that Mokichi Okada, the founder of the "Church of World Messianity" also advocated. Mr. Takizawa was healed by *'johrei'* by the 'Seimei-kyo' sect, a faction of the "Church of World Messianity."

There is another case in which an original Japanese hand-healing method became famous overseas and was then re-introduced to Japan. Many people may have heard of *'reiki',* which is officially called "Usui's Reiki Therapy." This therapy was developed by Mikao Usui (1865-1926), who is said to have acquired a certain healing talent when he fasted for a period of time in order to find the true meaning of his life, after working as a journalist, secretary of a politician, and many other professions. Today *'reiki'* is known all over the world, and is still spreading. This should be attributed to the fact that Mr. Usui invented ways of teaching how to acquire healing talent and how to develop leaders in the field. If Mr. Usui had intended to propagate the hand-healing method as a sort of religion, he may have not been successful even if he had had the desire to do so.

Shamanistic Techniques Revived in the Modern Age

Therapeutic touch is a technique confirmed by clinical testing to have healing effects. It was created by Dolores Krieger, who did scientific research on hand-healing methods as a practitioner of nursing science. After being compiled in a complete manual, an academic course on therapeutic touch was established in the graduate school of New York University in 1972. Since then, it has been widely introduced in other nursing schools and hospitals.

It is said that currently more than 15% of the nurses in the U.S. are adopting the method of therapeutic touch. Data has been gathered proving that the hand-healing method used in operations can reduce the amount of bleeding and stabilize the process of recovery.

As I have mentioned earlier, there are various types of hand-healing methods. Although the names differ, such as 'johrei', "therapeutic touch," or "spiritual healing," the basic procedures and results share many similarities.

We understand that these methods have also been practiced by shamans throughout history, and while there is proof that this type of therapy was practiced long ago, it may have been lost or abandoned without being well understood. Shamans developed healing talent naturally and each strived to use it in their own unique way, which resulted in masking the true mechanism. As a result the method of hand-healing was sometimes lost, or only continued within a single tribe. However, the hand-healing method is currently being studied in universities and specialized organizations, and it is hoped that our progress in science can help uncover the mechanisms of this method.

Why the Number of Cancer Victims is Growing

Alternative medicine will become a more and more important topic in Japan, as we reach the limits of modern medicine. Here I would like to discuss further the problems of modern medicine.

Medical expenses in Japan reached 34,808,400,000,000 yen in 2008, the largest amount spent in history. This constitutes 10% of the total income of our people. Within this expense, the cost of treatment for cancer accounts for as much as 12.8%.

Demographic research shows that malignant neoplasm, another name for cancer, was the greatest cause of death last year, and this has been the case for the last 30 years in Japan. The number of people who die of cancer has doubled since 1980, with eight million people around the world dying of cancer annually. Why has the rate of cancer increased so much?

As we all know, for every effect there is a cause. Causes of cancer are said to be genetic, stress-related, due to changes of lifestyle, bad habits, carcinogenic substances such as contaminated emissions, and so on. The risk of cancer due to bad habits and carcinogenic chemical substances has become significantly greater in recent decades.

I must add that cancer is not the only disease on the increase. Lifestyle diseases, intractable diseases, and other puzzling diseases have increased during the same time period, and although modern medicine seems to be improving its ability to cure disease, nevertheless the number of patients is increasing year by year.

One important thought comes to mind: how many diseases do we know the cause of and are there any cases in which the cause has been identified, but it is not actually what brought about the disease? I think that there are "causes of causes," perhaps more of an essential source of disease, and that this needs to be examined and methods of treatment explored.

Causes of cancer for example are thought to be due to genetic issues, bad habits, stress, and so on, which cause cancer cells to be generated and increase in number. However, there are people who do not suffer from cancer even if they are stressed out. There are also people who have immune cells that are efficient enough to kill cancer cells. Thus it does not seem that the same impact on the body brings about the same result. Additionally, there are many potential causes of cancer, which makes it difficult to identify the true causes of the disease.

Why Causes of Cancer Cannot be Specifically Identified

If we look deeply into the cause of cancer, many questions arise. Exactly why and how do carcinogenic substances generate cancer cells, and to what extent? Why couldn't the human body deactivate and eliminate these substances once they are taken in? Cancer may not only be caused by the carcinogens itself, but also by conditions of the body and soul. There is certainly a need to investigate the relationship between these elements.

The more we think about causes, the more questions arise. I believe it is fair to say that there are many cases in which it is difficult to identify the causal relation, because the human body is a complex machine affected by nature in still unexplained ways. And there are many other intractable diseases and puzzling diseases that modern medicine cannot even begin to find a cure for.

Effects do have causes. However, where the complex human body is concerned, it is impossible to connect the cause and effect perfectly, unlike in the field of physics where calculation and data analysis can clarify any process. We must also take into account that there are causes of causes, and that we may not understand the original source of a cause. Animate beings are different from inanimate objects and are much more difficult to understand. To identify the cause of a disease can be as difficult as figuring out the very mechanisms of life.

Natural Healing Power Advocated By Hippocrates

Alternative medicine focuses on activating a person's immunity or natural healing power, rather than identifying the cause of a disease. Adopting this focus can result in improved health and so it has prevailed and been developed in Europe and the U.S. Modern medicine is described as "symptomatic treatment," referring to the fact that it addresses the cause of a disease, while alternative medicine is described as "definitive therapy," indicating that it works with vital energy in order to reactivate the body's own healing mechanisms.

Looking at this issue from such a vantage point, it may seem that I am criticizing modern medicine, but that is not my intention. I admit that I am benefitting from modern medicine myself, and it is true that it can be very effective, especially when it comes to surgery or emergency treatments.

Even Hippocrates (around B.C. 460), known as the "father of medicine" or the "founder of medicine" and who developed what we call "natural medicine," acknowledged the importance of our natural healing power, and asserted that the human body tries to recover from damage by making use of it. Hippocrates examined the natural environment of patients and their symptoms and discovered that we can maintain our health and longevity by inspiring our natural healing energy. As previously indicated, daily bad habits, climate, and life environment cause various diseases. Therefore we must observe these phenomena and recognize the crucial symptoms in order to prevent disease or to improve our health.

Modern medicine, which has developed from Hippocrates' time, has altered to focus too much on the relationship between cause and effect rather than considering the human body as a living entity. It perceives the human body as a machine. I believe it has deviated from the original direction that

Hippocrates established, which focused more on strengthening our natural healing power.

Immunity Can Be Strengthened By Controlling Our Minds

Although, as I previously mentioned, it is difficult to identify the real cause of a disease, the Japanese word "byoki" (disease) implies the general cause of a disease. This word consists of two characters, which respectively mean "illness" and "mind." Japanese in the past said that "illness comes from an ill mind" and I do believe that whoever came up with characters for this word was a genius.

When we say "illness comes from an ill mind," we usually perceive "mind" as equal to "feeling." I believe experience and statistics can prove that illness mainly derives from negative feelings.

In fact, people who have lost their close relatives can die of deep sorrow, not being able to maintain their health. We know from the past of many cases in which mental shock brought about illness in people.

Oriental medicine is based on the "Gogyou" philosophy, which asserts that nature consists of five main elements: wood, fire, soil, gold, and water. According to this concept, human organs are also made up of these five elements, and if they become unbalanced, the body and soul become ill.

Each of these elements can be matched to human organs as follows; wood=liver, fire=heart, soil=spleen, gold=lung, and water=kidney. It is said that human emotions also derive from these organs: liver=anger, heart=joy/laughter, spleen=thought/consideration, lung=sorrow, and kidney=fear/surprise. And if any of these feelings become too acute, the function of each organ will be weakened. For example, a person who is always upset can damage the liver. If one is too joyful, the heart can be damaged, while one who thinks too much can damage the spleen. People who are always in sorrow may damage the lung, and those who are always afraid or fearful of something can damage their kidneys.

This is a credible belief that has been verified by statistical data over a long period of time. Oriental medicine is still largely based on this Gogyou philosophy today, and treats patients accordingly.

At the same time, modern medicine has discovered that emotions change the amounts of secreted hormones, which can affect the level of immunity. For example, if our body and soul experience stress, cortisol, which is a kind of adrenocorticotropic hormone, will be secreted from the hypothalamic area of the brain. Data shows that if too much cortisol is secreted, blood pressure or the blood glucose level will rise, which will result in a decline of immunity function. Cortisol prevents immune cells such as NK cells from activating, thus reducing the immunity of the body itself.

Cortisol is also called the "stress hormone" because its concentration in the blood increases when humans suffer from stress. In other words, a decrease in immunity depends on how we feel when we experience stressful situations. However, there are those who become depressed and those who do not, even if they experience the same level of stress.

As I explained previously, this theory is based on the same thinking as oriental medicine. If negative emotions such as anger, sorrow, or fear increase, our organs can be negatively influenced. This is where architectonics and modern science coincide, as verified by history.

Laughter Can Defeat Cancer

If the condition of our soul and our emotions can affect our organs, what will happen then if we maintain both in a positive condition? Many of you may conclude that a positive result will occur.

You are absolutely right. Currently research on boosting immunity through provoking laughter is a hot topic in the medical field.

There is experimental evidence that people who listened to "Rakugo," a Japanese traditional comic monologue, could activate NK cells and thus boost their immunity.

NK cells are called "natural killer cells," which are a kind of lymph corpuscle. They can kill tumor cells or viruses invading the body from outside. Although it is known that as many as 5,000 cancer cells may be created in a human body every day, we do not usually develop cancer because we are protected by immune cells, such as the NK cells. If we could activate these NK cells, we would not only be able to prevent cancer, but would also have the chance to cure the disease. Laughter is beginning to attract people's attention as an effective way of activating NK cells.

The latest scientific research has shown that laughter can activate certain functions of the brain. We know that approximately half of those who listened to Rakugo increased the amount of both alpha waves (brain waves detected when relaxed) and beta waves (brain waves detected when active). We also know that a certain hormone called beta-endorphin increases in the brain during laughing. This hormone, sometimes called the "pleasure hormone," increases blood flow and activates immune cells. NK cells are also activated with increased blood flow and smooth brain operation. Therefore, if you wish to get better grades or to work more efficiently, you should try to laugh deliberately.

Health Maintenance by Meditation

Meditation has long been acknowledged as an effective way to activate our brain or to reduce stress.

It has been adopted in Buddhism, Shugen-do, and Yoga, playing an important role in each of them. The main objective of meditation is to relax the body and the soul or to clarify the mind in order to encourage positive thoughts and feelings. Moreover, as it becomes possible to control negative emotions, such as anger or fear, we become better able to improve the conditions of our body and soul and thus improve our lives.

The alpha wave is a brain wave that is detected when we are meditating. It usually appears when our mind is stable and relaxed, indicating that our mind is in a good condition. We also have scientific data showing that blood pressure stabilizes if we continue meditating. This is because meditation can relax our mind, filling the mind with tranquility.

Dr. Deepak Chopra has recently introduced meditation as a way of bringing about miracles. He says that 20 minutes of meditation twice a day can change your life, bringing about the miracles you have always longed for. There is a similarity between Buddhism, Shugen-do and what Dr. Chopra is advocating in that people who meditate daily reach a higher spiritual level. In reality, things we do that are influenced by the invisible spiritual world can lead to visible phenomena in life including physical changes. This is also true of spiritual healing.

Two Meanings of the Saying *"Illness comes from an ill mind."*

According to mental situation, people may become ill or not. Therefore, it is important to alter the condition of your mind by effectively adopting laughter and meditation in your daily life. This encapsulates the meaning of the saying, "Illness comes from an ill mind." I would now like to consider a hidden significance of the same saying.

We have explained qi as the mind or emotion, but if we investigate the origin of qi, we learn that the outer part of the Chinese character means something vague and fluffy, such as a cloud; imagine steam, and you will understand what I mean. There are many words and expressions in Japanese that use this character: disease, liveliness, vigor, presence, motivation, to be careful, to be considerate, to be depressed, to be anxious, to be bothered, to be distracted, and so on. We have many everyday words that include the 'qi' character that are used without even being noticed. How would we explain them if a foreigner asks what they mean? Wouldn't it be difficult to answer clearly and precisely? Perhaps most of us are using these words but not knowing why we actually do so.

Chinese medicine, such as traditional herbal treatments, acupuncture and moxibustion, and Qigong therapy, on the other hand, treats qi as something invisible and flexible. Qi exists anywhere in the universe. It is also active inside the human body, and is said to cause problems if it stops flowing.

For example, if qi is stagnant in a room, indicating poor ventilation, fungus can be generated, food can go bad, and people staying there can suffer from difficulty in breathing or fatigue.

The same thing can be true of the human body. If qi is stagnating in the body, pain can be generated, possibly causing a certain kind of disease.

In traditional Chinese medical science they use methods like herbal therapy, acupuncture and moxibustion, Qigong therapy, and so on in order to improve the flow of qi. In traditional herbal therapy, herbs are given to patients for improving the balance of organs and the internal flow of qi. In acupuncture and moxibustion they stimulate acupressure points to adjust the flow of qi and the function of organs.

There are two different types of Qigong: external Qigong and internal Qigong. They are both methods for the Qigong doctor to utilize qi that is dispersed in the universe for improving the flow of the patient's qi. External Qigong is very similar to spiritual healing in that it makes use of cosmic energy to heal patients.

From this explanation, you can see that the concept of qi in traditional Chinese medicine embodies the saying, "Illness comes from an ill qi." In this case, qi is different from the mind or emotions but includes the mind and emotions. The difference is whether we take it macroscopically or microscopically.

If we try to understand qi macroscopically, described as 'prana' in Sanskrit, it is a vital energy that is present anywhere in the universe, or, in other words, as an energy that can create all beings. If we take qi microscopically, it is equivalent to the energy of the mind or emotions. Thus, macroscopically, qi as prana is the energy of creation while, microscopically, qi is the energy limited to the mind and emotions.

The saying "Illness comes from an ill qi" is correct both macroscopically and microscopically. We call our body and soul the "microcosmos." Our body and soul are the epitome of the universe, also being a part of it at the same time. Macro and micro are always related to each other, something that we must keep in mind at all times. This is a concept that is crucial to understanding the principles of spiritual healing.

Chapter 2
Causes of Illness

Excessive Amount of Information Prevents *qi* From Flowing Properly

As I mentioned in Chapter 1, it is difficult to track down the exact cause of a disease by only looking at its physical manifestations. If you only superficially examine the physical aspects of a disease, you will not be able to uncover the core cause.

On the other hand, if we keep the saying "Illness comes from an ill qi" in mind, we notice that a disease is caused by static qi, which is brought about by negative thoughts and emotions, as has already been explained.

There are external factors that cause our qi to stagnate, such as weather and the surrounding environment. When the qi or energy that we have inside us does not flow properly, many problems can occur.

According to my experience as a healer, I think we can roughly say that the cause of this static qi is "unmanageable information."

When we say "information," it is natural that we imagine pieces of knowledge that are either conveyed through newspapers and radios, or events that can be perceived by our senses. However, there is another meaning that has even broader implications:

"Information is everything that influences the action of an animate being. Lights and sounds in environment, biological signals such as uncontrollable nerves and hormones can all be regarded as 'information'." As we are always exposed to various types of information, this will cause all kinds of trouble if not properly managed.

Many definitions of information exist but they basically can be divided into two different types. We can call them "endogenous information" and "exogenous information."

Exogenous information refers to emotion, trauma, psychological wounds, and negative ideas.

The great variety of types of endogenous information can be listed as follows:

Material information, such as information from weather and the natural environment, information from communicative media (newspapers, magazines, books, radio, TV, letters, telephone, email, etc.), radio or electromagnetic waves, and immaterial information. If you cannot handle this endogenous information adequately, it may directly influence your organs negatively or affect your body, soul, and emotions, which may cause illness by preventing your qi from flowing appropriately.

Abilities That Can Be Lost Due to Excessive Information

People in modern society are indeed overloaded with information that cannot be properly managed by the body. There is an excessive amount of communication media that is now easily available. If we turn on the TV, the same information will be repeatedly transmitted. If we go out into the streets, we will be welcomed by a great variety of noises and commercial announcements. Our postboxes become full of mail and advertisement flyers if we are away from home for just a few days.

All this information creeps into us and causes stress to our nervous systems, sensory organs, and brains. We are gradually overwhelmed by all of this information and it eventually affects our body and soul. In some cases this excessive information can deprive us of our ability to maintain our normal lives as a human being.

As this process continues, our sensory organs will devolve without even giving us a sign. Whether we take it as a serious problem or not depends on each of us, but we must admit that it occurs.

For example, we acquire most of our information about the weather forecast from media such as TV, radio, and newspapers. However, in times when these types of media were not available, we sensed the change of weather through our sensory organs; our eyes, ears, and nose. This gives us an indication of how sensitive these organs once were.

While information has made our lives more convenient, human beings have been losing the ability to sense things directly. This is one of the most critical shortcomings of the modern information-oriented society. The devolution of our sensory organs implies that our ability to notice and avoid danger, or the ability to support ourselves is also devolving. Admittedly, the weather forecast is a minor example, but we still have to understand that many different problems can occur if we absorb too much information.

Negative Information is Inherent to Modern Society

It is not only communicative information that is increasing in volume. Every kind of information is increasing at a dangerous rate, gradually overwhelming the world with unmanageable information. Material information is equivalent to the material itself, and various kinds of products and substances such as chemical substances are distributed as science and industry continue to develop. It is no coincidence that, as the types of material increase in number, the types of illness and disease have increased as well.

Chemical substances include gas emissions, pesticides, and food additives. If these poisonous substances cannot be purified in the human body, they will change into carcinogens.

In reality, if we keep living in this kind of environment, stress that develops in our mind might affect our body. It may not only be the body itself that would be negatively influenced, but also our practical lives. Once we are accustomed to such an environment, it becomes difficult for us to notice how much of a negative influence it is imposing upon us. As I will explain in detail later on, spending a long period of time in a stressful life can sometimes cause serious problems.

Electromagnetic Waves as Possible Cause Heart Disease

Electromagnetic waves are included in the exogenous information inherent in modern society. Results of epidemiologic research show that, to a certain extent, electromagnetic waves can cause our health to deteriorate. The causal relation between these waves and diseases such as childhood leukemia, cancer, and brain tumors has been identified by researchers from our country and those from abroad.

Case of Kobe Café Owners Versus Sanyo Electric Corporation

The couple who owned a café in Kobe had been using an IH cooking heater. The chef developed heart disease and had to use a pacemaker. When the wife also suffered symptoms of irregular pulse, they changed the heater to a gas stove burner, which seemed to alleviate their symptoms.

A specialized organization conducted research requested by the couple and discovered that there are cases in which an electric current can flow into the human body under certain conditions. It was explained that the electric current could be conducted to the heater, as the handle was not insulated; a current would then pass through the body from the right hand to the left, which was in contact with the metal plate of the heater.

If we accept that the human body functions with electromagnetic energy, in other words biological electricity, it is easy to imagine that electromagnetic waves can weaken our vital power. Some biological electromagnetic waves play an important role in the release of hormones by sending information from the brain to appropriate organs. When this flow of electromagnetic waves is interfered with by exogenous electromagnetic waves, the nervous, endocrine, and immune systems will not function properly. This will upset homeostasis, which is an internal balance that supports the maintenance of our lives.

There is a growing danger that we are being increasingly exposed to electromagnetic waves, especially as IH devices and all-electric homes are becoming more and more common. We must also recognize the fact that many people frequently use cellular phones, which also use electromagnetic waves. Just recently there has been evidence found that indicates a link between extensive cellular phone use and brain cancer.

Electromagnetic waves occur not only at locations close to home electronic devices, but also where there are electric cables and wires. Even when electronic devices are turned off, an electric field will be created if they are still plugged in. In Europe, where grounding wires are normally installed, electric fields do not appear, at least not as much. However, in Japan, where grounding wires are very rare, any place with electronic devices or with electricity is exposed to electromagnetic waves.

The Invisible Threat of Electromagnetic Waves

Because invisible electromagnetic waves occur even in places that are separated by a wall, such as behind distribution boards, it is difficult for us to know whether we are affected or not and to identify a causal relationship between diseases and electromagnetic waves.

Mr. Kisho Kida, a healer of qi, points out the danger of electromagnetic waves negatively affecting our health in a book titled "A Miraculous Remedy" by Masayoshi Toyoda / Gentosha.

According to Mr. Toyoda, life in modern society can accelerate the accumulation of excessive electromagnetic energy in our bodies by factors such as stress, electromagnetic waves, ozone layer depletion, food contaminated by pesticides and chemical substances, and fossil fuel. This accumulation can cause cancer by damaging our genes. He realizes from his long experience of therapy that electromagnetic waves especially can cause serious health damage, which is mainly brought about by the damaging vibes that the waves cause.

The reason I decided to delve further into the subject of electromagnetic waves is because I believe it triggers one of the greatest negative influences of information that we are exposed to.

Currently the amount of information that human beings can handle is only about one 10-millionth of the quantity that exists. Electromagnetic waves especially affect delicate parts of our body without us noticing. It is fair to say that many of us living in modern society may be overexposed to electromagnetic waves and other information, which are already extending beyond the limits our bodies can comfortably handle.

Even if electromagnetic waves do not cause us to suffer from serious diseases, they can result in our becoming fatigued, easily irritated, and depressed. If this situation becomes worse and exceeds our limits we will easily develop a disease.

How We Can Protect Ourselves from Electromagnetic Waves

Though we must admit that electricity is indispensable in any aspect of our modern life, it is important to make use of it with correct knowledge about the risks. We must become aware of the importance of protecting ourselves from electromagnetic waves.

We may adopt the following methods to avoid the risk of electromagnetic waves;

- Use cellular phones only when you need to, and make a habit of keeping away from electric devices that are operating.

- Pull the plug out or attach a grounding wire on electric devices when they are not in operation. They will create electric fields if they are plugged in. (It is convenient to use power-save options so that you can easily switch devices off without unplugging).

- All-electric homes and IH cooking heaters are not recommended, since it is difficult to avoid the risks inherent in their use.

- Wear clothes made of natural materials, such as hemp, in order to avoid a build-up of static electricity. Shoe soles made of leather material function as a grounding wire.

Source of Disease is Invisible Energy

Electromagnetic waves are a kind of invisible information, but can be measured scientifically with monitoring devices. There are, however, types of information that we cannot measure, even with machines. This is information that only people with a special talent can feel and recognize.

In my career, working with many patients, there are times when I can just feel where the essential source of the problems lies. I would say that it is a conviction rather than a mere sense.

As I mentioned previously, whether a patient becomes ill or not depends on personal character and how well they can control their mind. There is, however, certain invisible information that can affect the patient's mind.

This is equivalent to the 'Yukai' (world of the dead) or energy that belongs to this world. It may be hard to understand, since it cannot be verified even by the latest scientific knowledge. I write about it in this book, because the influence of this type of energy is considerable. As a matter of fact, if we try to track down the cause of any disease or the background of–problems, we almost always arrive at this form of energy.

Yukai refers to a world that is full of the souls of dead people that could not reach the spiritual world as expected. This happens, for example, when the soul has a strong will to remain in this human world. Yukai results in negative forms of energy. Powerful emotions of sadness or anger, negative thoughts, and human obsessions are created by these souls living in Yukai.

People often assert that nothing remains after death, and that neither a spiritual world nor Yukai exist. Of course it is impossible to prove that they do exist.

There have been, however, many suggestions made about the possible existence of metempsychosis, made by people both inside and outside of our country. Metempsychosis implies that we may have lived a different life as another human being in the past, and that we might have been reborn many times.

Many children in the world have begun to talk in detail about places they have lived before and what they did before they were born. If we research the content of their stories, in some cases we find that the people they talk about actually existed in the past. There are quite a number of children that remember incidents that happened before they were born. In Japan, the director of Ikegawa Clinic, who used to be a manager of the Department of Obstetrics and Gynecology at Ageo Central General Hospital, introduces examples of children that talk about their previous life in his books and lectures.

People Vulnerable to Diseases Can Easily Connect With *Yukai*.

If we accept that *Yukai* and the spiritual world exist, it may be the *Yukai* that cause problems. The forms of energy in *Yukai* influence human beings in different ways. For example they can affect the body and soul, causing depression and integration disorder syndromes. It is possible to say that diseases and other problems that occur while living may be caused by influences from *Yukai*.

There are times when we are vulnerable to influences from *Yukai*, and it happens when we are connected to such forms of energy derived from when our thoughts and actions are negative. Vibrations produced by negative thoughts resonate with negative energy, just as waves of the same frequency resonate with each other.

In addition to material information negatively affecting the mind and body, so too will a room that is filthy with your belongings scattered. It is not only because the devastating atmosphere created by the chaotic environment makes you exhausted, but also because it attracts energy of the same type. If there is something rotten in your environment, energy with waves that resonate with oxidization and deterioration will be attracted. If your belongings are always scattered around, energy with waves that are scattered and dispersed will be accumulated. If you keep the environment in a disordered manner, you will continuously attract negative waves from *Yukai*.

Conforming a Room to *Yukai*.

The trend to organize a room making use of the concept of geomancy is somewhat similar to cleaning your room or toilet to bring in luck.

Looking at it from an energy point of view, this is very logical. If we keep the environment clean, the flow of qi will improve, which will allow you to maintain a pure space with goods and air that cannot be easily oxidized. Moreover, you will be able to spread your qi to every corner of the environment. As a result, strange and evil energy that does not fit the surroundings will not be able to come in, which will prevent bad incidents from happening.

Geomancy was originally a method developed in order to take in the positive energy of Mother Nature. For example, it requires you to make use of the energy of solar motion, landscape, and water movements in order to create a comfortable residential environment of your own. In terms of the sun, geomancy looks for a way to take in solar energy, which is strongest during the day. In order to accomplish that objective, it advises us to set the entrance in certain locations. It also advises us to avoid places where there is a flow of water nearby. There are certain recommended ways to choose locations, interiors and furniture, or make a good plan of a house. While every one of these is important, the most important factor is the flow of qi. If the qi of the house does not flow smoothly and remains still or stagnant, many kinds of problems may occur. It is necessary to absorb the qi of Mother Nature and find a way to keep it circulating all around the internal space of your house. If you do well in this process, you will be able to maintain a good healthy condition as well as a happy family. Geomancy has been developed to achieve such an environment so that the right energy is attracted.

As a representative example, we can think of prosperous temples and shrines that maintain a good qi. Shrines in particular have to be prepared every day to welcome God, which is a presence that consists of high-level energy. They have to clean the property, covering every single corner, and sprinkle water so as to keep the qi pure. Every element of the shrine, including the locations of trees and other natural elements in the background, are placed to take in the good qi of nature. Visitors' body and soul can only be purified when clean and pure qi is abundant, and thus spirits can come down with ease.

Places Where You Can Connect With Solemn qi Inside the House

In my experience it is important to maintain your environment in an ideal condition in order to prevent negative energy from affecting you, and to take in beneficial energy. I especially recommend you to be careful about how you treat water, in particular water in toilets and baths.

Where do you think it is easiest to connect to the spiritual energy in a house? Yes, it is the toilet and bath.

Although it is difficult to explain, toilets and baths have become special to me since I became sensitive to spiritual things.

In Shinto, we purify our bodies with fresh water or seawater while praying. Bathing also has the same ability to banish and reduce the power of evil thoughts or unnecessary energy. It is not only for pursuing comfort or relaxation. In Japanese, we have a unique expression, "*mizu ni nagas*," which literally means to wash away bad consequences with water. Just as it is implied in this context, water can wash away both physical things and unnecessary energy or emotions.

Baths and toilets are also said to exist in a different dimension from other rooms in the house; in fact they are places where we can refresh our mind. We know this instinctively, as we often go to the toilet just to refresh our mind without actually fulfilling the usual objective.

In Japan, we have a custom of making offerings of sake to the gods, and making a little pile of salt in front of the entrance to keep away negative energy. Both salt and sake are effective in banishing negative energy; in fact the actual effect not only keeps it away, but also adjusts the equilibrium points of energy. For example, when I take a bath with natural additives, not only does it help keep my body warm, but it also prevents people that I don't want to see from visiting me. Sometimes if I take a bath with some sake poured in, it makes me more comfortable talking with someone I don't know very well.

To tell the truth, I realized at one point that I could see and hear people in the invisible world. This happened especially when I stayed at hotels, when many strangers would come to see me at night. Once I began to fall asleep, I would have my leg pulled or feel a stimulation that resembled static electricity. However, this does not happen when I am together with my family. To avoid such unfavorable experiences I would have some sake or take a fine bath. Nowadays these experiences no longer happen to me.

The Best Way to Keep Away Bad Spirits

We can keep away bad spirits from *Yukai* by making use of salt or sake, but the most important thing is to keep your mind in good condition.

As I discussed in the previous chapter the Japanese saying, "Illness comes from bad qi," means that we can both cause illness and prevent or cure diseases such as cancer by controlling our emotions. The biggest reason for this is that the condition of our mind changes the waves of our qi, allowing energy of the same frequency to come together.

Thus by laughing, we can become cheerful and positive and so are able to release negative energy naturally. Since positive and optimistic feelings are essentially different from those of sadness, anger, or hatred, negative energy will not be attracted to you, which makes it possible to keep it away.

Another significant solution to avoiding negative energy is to protect ourselves from electromagnetic waves; negative energy accumulates where electromagnetic waves are powerful. As I have already explained, in addition to the damage that can be caused by electromagnetic waves, we must also consider the influence of negative energy caused by bad spirits. It is vitally important to avoid being affected by electromagnetic waves.

Chapter 3
Principle of Spiritual Healing

Healers That Can Carry Away Negative Energy

There are many different types of spiritual energy; God, for example, represents an ultimate higher dimension. There are others that are beneficial to us, such as the spirits that protect nature, but there are also types that are harmful to us. These harmful types bring about disease and accidents, and represent forms of energy from Yukai. Since these amplify negative energy, those who are exposed to it can become depressed or extremely upset.

Because I am not a specialist in this field, I must admit that I do not have precise knowledge about categorizing spiritual energy, but I am able to sense these types of energy. I will explain about power spots in later chapters; there are places that are strongly influenced by these types of spiritual energy.

I advise everyone to avoid being exposed to negative energy. If it is impossible to do so, you should ask specialized healers to help you. In cases where negative energy is causing problems, the best way to solve the problem is to ask for spiritual healing treatment.

The Mechanism of Spiritual Healing

I will now explain the mechanism of spiritual healing, but first of all I must explain the presence of spiritual energy, which I find very important as a professional healer. Spiritual energy is the energy that functions as the principle of spiritual healing.

This form of energy is generally called a guardian spirit; such a guardian spirit is a presence that protects our lives. Each one of us, without exception, has this spirit.

Some people may be suspicious about why I bring this subject up in the context of healing. Some may also doubt the existence of guardian spirits, since it is not a presence that has been verified, unlike Yukai and the spirits that reside there. However, the truth is that a guardian spirit actually plays the most important role in the spiritual healing world.

The reason is simple: I am not the one who is healing the patient directly; rather it is a form of energy like the guardian spirit that is actually doing the job.

Although the mechanism of spiritual healing has not yet been discovered, Mr. Harry Edwards, who I introduced earlier, talks about this principle by discussing a healing spirit that resembles the guardian spirit. He says,

"When the human mind that conforms to spiritual intelligence radiates a certain thought, the spirit guide reads the intent and manages to cure the physical unbalance."

Mr. Edwards says it is the spiritual guide, a form of spiritual intelligence, that actually heals the disease. The healing process is inspired by the healer, who can communicate the problems to the spirit guide, who in turn stimulates the natural healing ability of the patient's body. As explained in previous chapters, there are different types of healing methods and these processes can be categorized as direct treatment and remote treatment.

As Mr. Edwards explains,
"The essence of direct treatment depends on the relationship between the healer and the patient, or between the healer and the instructor. The healer's sense of responsibility and compassion towards the patient encourages the soul on both sides to become one. Thus the healer and the patient will be mentally connected with each other, which will also comingle the spirits of the two."

With a few exceptions, my healing method is quite similar to that of Mr. Edwards.

Characteristics of Healing Represented by Remote Treatment

The similarity between Mr. Edward's explanation of remote treatment and mine increased my confidence in my method. Mr. Edwards' remote healing is explained as follows:

"Put simply, remote treatment is a healing process delivered to a patient remotely; the healer is not personally known to the patient. Requests for remote treatment can be accepted both verbally and by written application. A healer that is contacted for a remote treatment will try to connect with a spirit guide and communicate all information that they possess together with the wishes of the patient. The healer will submit to the spirit guide, relinquishing any materialistic interest from his mind. ... The healer then waits until the spirit guide contacts the patient. This action may be difficult for us to understand, even though it is clearly happening in real life. The spirit guide can find and reach the patient quite easily. There is much proof that supports spiritual healing, demonstrating that contacts are being realized and that patients cannot be cured without this kind of process. Most of the healing I do is based on remote treatment, approximately 1,000 cases per week. The spirit guide identifies the cause of disease and primarily focuses on eliminating it. Then it goes on to free the patient from symptoms brought about by stress." (All comments of Mr. Edwards are extracted from "A Guide to Spirit Healing" by Harry Edwards).

While Mr. Edwards uses the term "spirit guide," I maintain that my guardian spirit contacts other spiritual presences, according to the requirements, and that is them who cure the patients. In other words, the guardian spirit calls the spirit guide to do their jobs. This process is different from that described by Mr. Edwards.

The fact that I have many cases of remote treatment is similar to Mr. Edwards' situation. Remote treatment and direct treatment are the same in mechanism; both involve a spirit guide as a go-between. The process may be difficult to understand because in most cases I don't actually see the patients personally. The fact that remote treatment and direct treatment brings about the same consequence may imply that I am not utilizing my own personal energy in the process of healing patients.

This is different from other hand-healing methods or acupuncture because it does not involve direct contact with patients, such as pressing on acupressure points to urge qi to flow. It is impossible to determine the exact process involved since the treatment is actually done by the spirit guide. This is why spiritual healing is mysterious and difficult to understand.

Healing Talent Awakened While Working as a Resident Doctor

On reflection, my talent did not appear out of the blue. It was already being utilized when I first noticed it, especially after I became a doctor.

I already had had special childhood experiences, such as seeing prophetic dreams or spirits. It was when I worked as a trainee doctor that I began to realize I had special talent in this area.

While working as a resident doctor at a university hospital, one night I was responsible for a late-shift, and since patients tend to pass away from midnight to dawn, I was quite nervous at the possibility of witnessing a moment of death. Unusually, I never did experience such a situation; patients never passed away when I was in charge, while many would when other doctors had to stay overnight.

I often held my hand against the diseased part of the patient's body without even intending to do so. Sometimes I couldn't help focusing on those illnesses, only to find that those patients would then look much better and begin to steadily recuperate.

Thus I sensed long ago that I possessed a special talent. When I opened my own clinic and began to see many patients, I began to understand more about this talent. Gradually, I became able to detect the negative waves of the patients, and could no longer resist making efforts to cure them.

I remember when my grandmother became seriously ill. I rushed to see her, held her hand for a while, and she recovered dramatically, being able to talk as usual. She was able to live another two years after this incident.

Something mysterious happened when my grandmother passed away. That night, when I was enjoying a dinner with my wife at a Chinese restaurant in Nishi-Azabu, I heard my grandmother's voice. She said, "Now I'm about to die." At that moment, I didn't understand what was happening, but the next morning my parents phoned to say my grandmother had passed away around seven o'clock the previous evening. I assume that my grandmother didn't realize that she had died. But after she actually passed away I believe she understood what had happened and came to greet me.

It was through experiencing these kinds of episodes, that I came to realize my special healing abilities.

Process of Dr. Minamu's Spiritual Healing

In order to start my original healing method, I must free my mind so that I can connect with the spirits.

Then I must adjust the waves by holding my hand against the patient's belly button, since that is where the energy is collected. If the patient is suffering from a certain illness, such as cancer, I may hold my hand against the affected part of the body for a while.

After that, the process begins involuntarily. The guardian spirit proceeds with the healing process by itself.

Although it varies with each individual, those with serious illnesses feel some tingles in the affected parts of their bodies. The more serious the illness is, the stronger this tingle will be. If I were to explain this situation with qi, I would conclude that it must be flowing in a strange direction.

If healing is done directly, the tingling of the affected area would soften and no further treatment would be necessary.

When healing is done remotely, I will imagine the affected area of the patient while staring at a name card. For example, if there is a problem with the liver, I would focus on the image of the liver. The process that follows would be the same as that of direct treatment, meaning that the spirit guide proceeds with healing actions. When this process is over, a soothing feeling will result, letting us know that no further treatment is needed for the day. Thus there is no real difference between direct healing and remote healing. The only difference is that in direct healing the patient is physically in front of the healer and can have a unique feeling on the affected area.

Healing is a Collaboration With the Spirit Guide

We also understand that a spirit guide exists to cure people by listening to the patients' stories. Once, when I was healing a patient who had breast cancer, she told me that she clearly saw a man standing in front of her with a beard and who looked like a doctor aged approximately 50 years old from the Edo era. She said that she could sense these spirits from time to time.

Although I personally have never seen a spirit guide, five or six years ago I did have a chance to see my guardian spirit. She was a vigorous woman wearing a kimono, possibly from the Kamakura era. When I first met her I intuitively knew that she was protecting me as a guardian spirit.

When this woman appears, she is usually dancing and energetically uttering a Buddhist chant. The dance is similar to what we used to call the "Chanting Dance" in the Heian era, spread in the Kamakura era by a monk whose name was "Ippen." He had learned this method from another monk named Kuya. Since Ippen and the Buddhist chant have a strong relationship with spiritual healing, I will discuss them further in detail later.

This woman who seems to be my guardian spirit is not healing patients herself. She is requesting other spirits that are familiar with medical knowledge to heal my patients. I do however sense sometimes that this woman's powerful energy is supporting me while I am working on spiritual healing.

The Key to Becoming a Good Healer is to Free One's Mind

Although I am not quite sure why my guardian spirit works in such a manner, I do believe that it is following its instincts by supporting the talent that it is in charge of. It must be doing its best to make sure that my talent contributes to help as many people as possible since I have been gifted with the ability to heal. I believe that it was my destiny to become a healer.

I also began to notice while seeing many patients that there are certain situations in which the guardian spirit can work effectively.

This tends to happen when I am most able to free my mind. Such a situation occurs when I have almost lost consciousness and cannot even remember what I was trying to do. In reality, I do not lose consciousness entirely, because that would prevent me from focusing on my job, but at that moment my desires and thoughts are gone and I cannot judge things as usual either.

To put it in another way, the guardian spirit does not function when I don't have a free mind. If I tried to heal the patient with my own might, it would not be possible.

When I focus on healing a patient, I don't think about which spirit is actually doing the job. I do have a slight involvement in solving the problem but basically just let everything happen naturally.

Mr. Harry Edwards discusses this kind of feeling in his book titled "Spiritual Healing." He says, "Healers conform to the spirit guide by depriving themselves of all materialistic interests." He also says,

"Healers should always be aware of themselves. The term – mental concentration – usually means to develop spiritual capability; however, this is not a correct interpretation. What is truly necessary is not mental concentration but freedom of the mind."

Whether a person can free their mind determines if they can perform well as an excellent healer.

This is why I focus strictly on pushing my own thoughts aside; it is something I do naturally. At times when my mind tends to be distracted, I remember to take a deep breath or practice yoga for an hour or so. These actions are part of the process of preparation. Once I begin with the healing treatment, I try not to make any effort; I do not feel anything while I focus on healing. The patient, on the other hand, says "I am sweating" or "tears are dropping," but I do not notice that these things are happening during the process.

The Guardian Spirit's Support Becomes Greater Once the Healer Frees His Mind

Whether one can free his mind has become an important issue, not only for a healer to work effectively, but for us all to perform well in various aspects of life.

In my case, if I can attain the ideal condition of freeing my mind, I experience wondrous synchronicity and positive events. Synchronicity refers to the fact that I can acquire necessary information right on time and that I can see the desired people whenever I need to.

For example, though I am fond of the game of Go, it is almost impossible for me to win if I focus too much on victory. I win when I sit back and stay calm, although it is hard to understand why this happens.

I also pick up money in the streets a couple of times a week. Although the amount of money is usually small, such as one yen or 100 yen at a time, I may pick up money a few days in a row. I recall that every time I find money my mind is set in a free condition.

When I receive messages from the guardian spirit, I have my mind free too.

Approximately ten years ago I was going to take one of my staff to a restaurant to have dinner, when I heard the voice of my guardian spirit saying, "wear something green." Since I had a blue uniform on, I swiftly changed my clothes and shoes to green ones. The day after this change of clothes I experienced something very interesting. Three patients in a row, all called 'Midori,' which means green in Japanese, came to my clinic. It was the first time I had experienced such a phenomenon, and it may be the last. I assume that my guardian spirit desperately wanted to give me that important piece of information: to keep green clothes on. One or two years ago, my guardian spirit started to tell me that I should wear purple. However, I choose to follow that message in private since it is difficult to do so at my clinic.

Incidentally, green and purple are the colors that monks tend to wear; it is said that these colors have waves that can connect with the spiritual world.

Although nothing special occurred just because I changed the color of my clothes, green is a color that has a certain healing effect on us. It seems that my patients can come to my clinic with ease, and I am thankful for support of all kinds. I have no doubt that my guardian spirit has a lot to do with the fact that I am doing well as a spiritual healer. That is why I am determined to give priority to the messages that I receive from my guardian spirit.

There are also times when I realize that my guardian spirit is helping me when I am drunk, though it is different from a mind-free condition. I would imagine that many of you have had an experience whereby you found yourself lying in a garden close to your home. You would find bags and other precious belongings with you, even if you don't have exact recall of what happened. We may say that this type of thing happens because we are experiencing a condition similar to a free mind when we are drunk, which makes it easier for our guardian spirits to help us.

Miraculously Saved From a Serious Accident

I have also experienced times when I felt that my guardian spirit helped me. The following two episodes both impressed me.

It was in my freshman or sophomore year in university when I went to Karuizawa with my friends, driving on the highway in two different cars. I was driving one of the cars at a speed of 160 kilometers per hour, which was quite normal for me. My friend in the other car took the exit for a service area before Higashi-Matsuyama because he was scared of the speed. It was right after he exited that a serious accident occurred.

The car in front of us stopped abruptly, and I had to brake hard. However, I was not in time. I pulled the steering wheel sharply to the side, which made the car crash into the side of the road and turn over; the car was smashed up. Our friends in the other car thought we were all dead, but we were all actually safe without suffering any injuries. It was a miracle.

Thinking back about this accident, I realize that we were lucky to have our friends exit right before it happened. It was also fortunate that we all had our seatbelts on; I was especially lucky because I normally did not put on my seatbelt. The conditions were also on our side as the soil on the side of the road was openly exposed.

The moment the crash happened, I remember seeing it in slow motion; I clearly sensed that I was in a special situation. Although it was not so apparent at the moment, I did feel that a certain presence was trying to protect me.

As it was a serious accident, people that witnessed it were very surprised to see that we came out of the smashed car unharmed. My friend took me to the hospital close by, telling me that there was no way I could be uninjured after being in such a big accident. However, the results of medical examination showed that I was perfectly all right.

One of the local people told me afterwards that the vicinity was famous for having fatal accidents because the road was constructed on top of a cemetery. To ruin a cemetery certainly has consequences for the spiritual world. Although dead people do not reside in the cemetery, it is where we communicate with the dead (almost like looking into a school yearbook). Therefore it is natural that the spirits would refuse to have the cemetery destroyed.

On a positive note, I was able to buy a new car since I had insurance.

September 11 Divided Life and Death

We know that guardian spirits are supporting us all the time. In my case, however, it is hard to count how many times they saved my life. Here I would like to introduce another unforgettable incident I experienced.

This was on the 11th of September of 2001, when that horrible act of violence occurred at the World Trade Center in New York.

I was staying in New York on business at the time, and commuting to the Center everyday in the morning at the same time. However, on that particular day, I woke up late, which prevented me from reaching the site at the actual moment of the attack.

I was living in an apartment on the 25th floor of a building located within a two or three minute walk from the World Trade Center, but could not see that building from my window. Though I do not turn on the TV often, I did so that morning and saw an airplane fly into the building. At first I thought it was a movie or something of that sort, but was tremendously shocked when I understood that it was a reality.

That day, if I had gone to the Center at the same time as usual, I would not have been able to write this book. On reflection, I know that I was saved because I woke up late, but I cannot help believing that my guardian spirit helped me survive. At the same time, I realize how fragile our lives are, and that human beings cannot live alone without the help of others around them.

Geniuses Know How to Free Their Minds

Once I am able to free my mind, it becomes easier for me to heal people. Listening and reading about those who are called "geniuses" in other fields, I realize that they are also experiencing a mind-free condition.

There are many athletes that have experienced such situations. The best golf players, baseball players, and soccer players must be freeing their minds at moments when they positively believe that they will do well. We often call this kind of condition a "zone," in which we feel that our body is loose and flexible. At that moment, our guardian spirits can easily lend us a hand, because we have no control over ourselves.

Athletes tend to find themselves in this special condition because there are many moments in which they have no time to think, such as a judo player trying to throw the opponent in a serious match. If they are too conscious about what is happening, they will lose the match. If they have a free mind, on the other hand, they can make a brisk move before their opponent does. Athletes are often able to sense this atmosphere by training themselves.

Athletes often have special guardian spirits that have sharp and unique techniques; they are more like monks in that sense. However, Matsui, who is a famous baseball player, resembles a popular politician. We can see from this case that the athlete's characteristics and how they perform are influenced by their guardian spirits. Though a previous life is different from a guardian spirit, the famous Ichiro was a monk.

Despite the fact that people may not notice it, the experience of a loose and flexible body at critical moments is shared among all of us.

Inventors are those who frequently experience this condition. We are also free of mind when we are inspired. In that particular moment, we are receiving hints from heaven or the spiritual world. In other words, inventors are not inventing things by themselves, but connecting themselves with these worlds in order to give birth to innovative products.

Musicians are also similar to inventors in this sense.

Many composers who have created eternally beloved works claim that they did not create the ideas by themselves, but just received inspiration from heaven. Mozart, who was called a prodigy, could hear all of the scores in his mind at once with an instant inspiration. All he had to do was to physically write it down on a piece of paper afterwards.

Tatsuro Yamashita, a famous pop singer in Japan, is another recent example. As he has commented himself, his song "Christmas Eve" was created without preparing a clear concept. It was made without being conscious about the process of creation; this is a good example of channeling oneself with heaven. These types of songs become big hits, enjoying long-term sales.

As for vocalists, Misia should be introduced as a good example. Although we must admit that she has a special talent, her voice is more like a gift from heaven. Since we are originally born with a certain type of voice, there is little we can do to change what we are given. However, we must make efforts to make full use of what we are gifted.

Fortune Can Be Controlled By Freeing Your Mind

We have witnessed many cases in which composers and vocalists become famous with smash hits, but disappear after a short period of success. They also have waves of good times and bad times. These things happen because they are distorted by desire and egoism. They concentrate too much on how they want to create their works, which results in cutting the relationship with guardian spirits and losing the opportunities to be inspired. However, if they could still be strong when they start to run out of money and regain their selves, they will be able to have support from their guardian spirits again. On the other hand, if they cannot, they will lose their chance to be supported. As we often say there is a 12-year cycle of biorhythm. We tend to be obsessed with our desires and egoism every few years, losing successful times during these periods. But if we can control our desires, we will be able to maintain a good condition of life regardless of this biorhythm.

Use is also made of a free mind at the level of company management and manufacturing factories.

Those who must develop new technology or those who hold an important social responsibility often know that little can be done if they focus too much on working only for themselves.

The founder of Nintendo, a manufacturer that makes both hardware and software for the game industry, named the company believing that "leaving it to heaven" was the best way to cope with things ('Ninten' has this literal meaning in Japanese). He practically let the destiny of the company be decided by heaven. This story reminds us about the connection between the spiritual world and ourselves.

I believe that the famous brain surgeon who often appears on TV, and is acknowledged to be one of the most technologically advanced in his field, also has had a lot of support from heaven. All doctors who perform well in the medical field are more or less helped by an invisible power, in addition to the actual techniques and skills they have. The brain surgeon I just mentioned was born in the Meiji Shrine, which is known as a spiritually special location.

Besides musicians, other artists may also experience a mind-free condition.

Monet is a typical example. The fact that he often sat in the same position drawing the same water lilies in his later stages of life may indicate that he was already freeing his mind.

Shiko Munakatta, a famous sculptor, carves out his works with the power of heaven, not his own. This means that his guardian spirit is doing the job. His art works have the power to change surrounding negative waves to positive ones and radiate waves of very high energy. A replica of his work is placed in the doctor's room at my clinic too.

Ryu Murakami is a good example of a recent modern artist. His work may not seem to be pieces of art, but investigated in detail we find that there are some that have been created by a power from heaven. Although we can see that there are commercial ones and those that resemble pop art, we also find works that seem to be created with power coming from a different dimension. Those who notice this will buy them even when they are very expensive. These types of works will last for a long period of time.

Reviewing all of these examples, we can say that it is important to free the mind in anything that we try to do. Once we become free in our mind, the invisible powers of the spiritual world can easily be invoked. This is the basis of a healer who must cure patients with the method of spiritual healing. Our treatment will become even more effective if the recipients stay in the same condition with us, and this is also true for those who wish to enhance their talent, succeed in either their work life or in love life, and make their dreams come true.

Hints for Becoming Free of Mind

How can we become free of mind? I would like to introduce some concrete examples.

In Japan, we often say, "pray for god in difficulties." There is a hint hiding in this saying.

Buddhism suggests that there are two different ways to save people from bitterness in life and of concerns. One is to pray for others to help, and another is to make things happen yourself. The Jodo sect, whose principle is to save people by guiding them to paradise with the help of Amidanyorai, is a typical example that can be categorized as the former. In fact, here we can find one of the mechanisms for becoming free of mind.

Amidanyorai was originally a Hozo bodhisattva who trained himself and became the enlightened one. He was said to be a most merciful nyorai, one that prayed for the salvation of all. The Buddhist chant "Namuamidabutsu" literally means "I will dedicate myself to Amidanyorai." In the Jodo sect, everybody chants like this in order to reach paradise.

Muneyoshi Yanagi, who is the master of Shiko Munakata, and known as the father of folk art movements, wrote a book titled "Namuamidabutsu." This is a collection of articles that he serialized in a magazine called "Daihourin." Muneyoshi, who was influenced by Ippen, the founder of the Jodo sect, wrote about Ippen like this:

"Nobody can resign oneself without following the principle of Namuamidabutsu. None of the six characters of Namuamidabutsu signify human beings and nyorai. This indicates that the only thing that exists is Namuamidabutsu. The six characters represent the place where human beings completely abandon themselves. It is also where the Amida is risking the Amida itself. Thus human beings and Amidas are both presences that are merely a step to going on to the next stage of Myogo. Human beings and Amidas exist on the premise that Myogo is given."

Although this is a difficult idea to understand, we may find clues in Ippen's words.

"None of the six characters represent life nor death. We may prove that no life exists merely by pronouncing this word." This means that there is a key to overcoming life and death and attaining moksha in the characters that signify Namuamidabutsu. Yanagi adds the following at the end of this paragraph:

"In fact the word Namuamidabutsu represents attaining moksha. The principle of the Jodo sect is concentrated in these six characters."

This means that if you keep chanting "Namuamidabutsu" with great concentration, you will be able to free your mind and connect with Buddha in the spiritual world. The word Namuamidabutsu originally had a special energy. We can say that it is similar to the mechanism of chanting a mantra in order to relax oneself.

We Can Also Free Our Minds By Repeating Menial Labor

What Muneyoshi Yanagi intended in his book "Namuamidabutsu" is revealed in his folk art movement.

Discovering high artistic quality in art works made by people that are not well known, he classified them as the highest ranked among tea utensils. He says that they could not have been ranked the highest if they were not works of folk art.

Why did he find such value in folk art?

From the following sentences in his book "Introduction to Folk Art," we can see his intention has a similarity to the spirit of Namuamidabutsu.

"Hundreds of the same product can be made in a day. Since this is done by divisional collaboration, the same shapes, the same patterns, and the same colors are repeated. Although many may detest this monotony, progress in techniques can be expected. Once these techniques are completed skills easily become forgotten. Artists keep moving their hands, forgetting about what they meant to create or draw. At this point there is no hesitation. Nobody is sticking to their consciousness. This repetition is what pushes ordinary people to a level of experts."

We see that in composing or in any other creative processes, we cannot make something of good quality if we think too much about our objectives. As Yanagi says, "Artists keep moving their hands, forgetting about what they meant to create or draw." We need to have a free mind for us to create valuable art works. This may indicate that we are channeling ourselves with heaven without even noticing it. Yanagi also mentions in the following sentences that people who work with a free mind are somewhat similar to people with virtue.

"Let us look back to what we have learned from our early years about virtue and religion. What we have been taught is all correct, because they are the words of many saints and sages. According to this preaching, it is better to be austere than to be rich, if you want to abide by the intentions of God. It is said that it becomes more difficult to reach heaven if you are wealthy. Modest people are better accepted than those with excessive pride and egotism. It is because they combine well with virtue. We must keep calm rather than behave abnormally. Those who can keep a tranquil mind are always respected by others. A free mind contributes more than techniques. Those who live in seclusion do ill, while those who work hard will never be given times of sorrow."

Yanagi insists that to be free of mind is the most important thing in both creating artwork and chanting Namuamidabutsu.

Locations Where We Can Easily Become Free of Mind

Whether it is sport, art, or any kind of hobby the best way to become free of mind is to proceed in your actions without being trapped in your thoughts.

Whether it is baseball or soccer that you are involved in, when your body is moving on its own, independent of your thoughts, the power of a free mind is strengthened.

Even when you are playing a game of Go, once you are used to the rules, it is better not to think too much. Then you may be able to see the best places to put your stones.

It is often said that the Go board represents the universe. There are moments when Go players find paths that connect with values of life or a world of a different dimension on the board. This experience is the real thrill of Go. The reason why politicians and company presidents are fond of Go is because they are inspired in many ways. Incidentally, there are many words that we usually use which derive from the Go game. "To sacrifice a stone," "a bad place to put," "decide black or white," or "give due respect." All of these traditional Japanese expressions originally come from the game. Go is the epitome of life itself, and it is a good way for training a free mind.

As I have already mentioned a couple of times, practicing Yoga and methods of respiration and meditation are other ways to become free of mind. I do Yoga myself, and find it especially effective in that it can easily help stop my flow of thinking. This can be done by anybody even without a strong will. Since it is quite easy to find instructive DVDs of good quality these days, you may want to make use of them. As in the respiration method of Yoga, if you take deep breaths, especially focusing more on blowing out slowly, it will help you to have a free mind. You should also practice Yoga as a way of freeing yourself from too much information.

There are certain locations where you can easily become free of mind. These days the media now pick up on so-called "power spots," which are the places where you can actually feel various effects. As I will explain in detail later on, the biggest role of power spots is to help us free our minds.

A shortcut to become mind-free is to take a bath. Although you cannot be completely free of mind, I would recommend taking a relaxing bath, especially if you are in a stressful job. If you also pour a bit of salt into the bath it will help keep away bad qi.

When you are in a bad condition, the best solution is to sleep well. If you can induce yourself into a deep sleep, that is when you can be most free of mind. If you have caught a cold, you should go to bed rather than eating nutritious food.

A method to learn from guardian spirits

When you are sleeping, you are not only resting your body and soul, but you are also channeling yourself with the spiritual world. Even if you think you are not able to free your mind, you are actually doing so with a good sleep. The reason why inventors come up with good ideas after falling asleep or waking up in the morning is because then they are free of mind without actively using their brains. They can receive hints from guardian souls by connecting themselves to the spiritual world.

On the other hand, if you think too much or if you are caught in negative thoughts, it is difficult to free your mind. You must stop your emotions in order to reach the ideal condition.

When we are trapped in deep thoughts, it is sometimes hard to make our way through. At these times, we tend to create a bad image of ourselves and end up making things worse.

If you know that you tend to think too much, you need to give things up. Try letting go of your concerns and believe that tomorrow is another day. Then you will be able to create an environment where others around you can do their best. "Others around" means people in the spiritual world.

Once you let go of your concerns, your desires and egotism will disappear. Those without desires are strong. If you can get rid of your desire for health and wealth, you will become stronger than you are now.

If you are always hoping that you become healthy, that obsession may prevent you from becoming healthy in real life.

People who are said to be lucky or those who keep a healthy condition know how to free their minds. No matter how much information you take in, you will be all right if you can keep a free mind. It is because your guardian spirit will help you.

As I have repeated many times, when you still have your egotism, guardian spirits cannot do their job. When you are free-minded, on the other hand, your guardian spirits can be very effective.

A Life In Connection With Your Guardian Spirit

Training your guardian spirit is a part of your daily life. Sleeping, bathing, thinking ... all of them are what you do every day. Eating is also a good training.

Eating without thinking is another good way of training. As we see many monks focusing on eating what they have in front of them. It is a pure method of training. Some say that if you concentrate on eating, sometimes scenery from the original land of the food appears in your mind. Sommeliers also experience the same thing. I've heard that scenery of a vineyard in South America had appeared if the glass of wine that a sommelier had was made in that part of the world. This is a case in which good concentration brought about a free mind and a special sense. We may be able to call this a type of psychic power.

When we listen to music or when we watch videos, if we can free our minds and concentrate, a new world of high dimension can be seen. If we can spend our days in such a manner, we will be able to have a healthy and happy life.

I began writing about the principle of my spiritual healing and ended up discussing how to spend our daily life. What I want to emphasize is that the principle of both aspects is the same.

In the next chapter, I will explain more concretely about the principle of spiritual healing with examples based on actual experiences.

Chapter 4
The Basics of Spiritual Healing

Regardless of the differences in symptoms, the methods adopted in spiritual healing are basically the same.

In the previous chapter we briefly mentioned the different methods of healing. I would now like to go over the key points again for your understanding.

First of all, those who request spiritual healing must fill in a questionnaire. We use this information to form an image of the patient. If we judge that further information is necessary, we may ask additional questions. In some cases, the healing process begins when the questionnaire is filled in. This is because the spirit guide can begin the treatment as soon as it receives information about the patient through me.

In direct treatment, I will sit in front of the patient and focus on freeing my mind so that the spirit guide can make use of its power. Then I will hold my hand against the patient's stomach for a while. This is when energy begins to flow into the affected area.

It is not an intentional but a natural process. My mind is gradually cleared out and reaches a point where I am almost completely mind-free. When the patient feels that the qi is flowing much more smoothly than before, it implies that sufficient energy has been flowing, and that the treatment has been successful.

In remote healing, energy flows to the part of the body that comes to my mind. I also concentrate on the supposedly weakened part by using information acquired from the questionnaire. However, in most cases the spirit guide has already grasped the problem and begun the treatment. Then I just imagine the energy flowing while freeing my mind. Just as with direct healing, the treatment would be over when the patient feels a sense of refreshment.

The time it takes for a treatment depends on the spirit guide. If the spirit guide judges that more time is necessary, it may take considerable time, depending on the patient's condition. The longest it will usually take is 10 to 20 minutes; the shortest is approximately 5 minutes.

Patients may feel that they are being healed right after they hand in the questionnaire. Many of them say that they are free from pain or feel better after 24 hours; I do not know why it takes a day before they actually sense the difference. There are many patients who feel that their bodies heat up or sweat a great deal during the treatment.

Although the patient's progress depends on the level of pain and symptoms, minor illnesses such as backache and hernia can be healed after one or two treatments. On the other hand, if it is a serious condition, such as cancer, they should take treatment once every 7 to 10 days, and repeat it at least 10 times. In these cases it is very important that they continuously maintain a good physical condition without pain or serious symptoms.

Pain and symptoms are normally memorized in the brain or the affected area. Therefore, even if the patient's condition is improved, this memory can cause the same illness to reoccur again. This is especially true if the disease is cancer. Frequent treatment is required because cancer cells can easily multiply. If the patient can take multiple treatments in a short time, the improved condition will be memorized and the illness will be steadily healed. It is therefore, important for patients to take treatment repeatedly until the disease is irreversibly healed.

Mental disorder is also a serious disease like cancer and requires almost the same amount of treatment at the same frequency.

Radium Stones Catch Attention

The symptoms of those who come to consult me vary a great deal. I give them advice according to their unique cases, but I sometimes give them radium stones if they wish. The stones support them in maintaining healthy conditions.

Radium stones emit a low level of radioactivity, which is said to bring about what is called a "hormesis effect." The Hormesis effect is a concept formulated by Thomas D. Luckey in 1982, and basically proposes that a low level of radioactivity activates organic functions. Radioactivity itself is harmful to human beings, but if the quantity is low, it can positively stimulate the body. It also helps improve immunity, which is an effect that many professors and medical specialists around the world are studying as a potential new method for curing disease.

Radon hot springs are known to have a hormesis effect. Radon is an element that is generated when radium becomes disrupted. If we put radium in a bath, we can expect the same effect as from a radon hot spring. This will help curing cancer, depression, integration disorder syndrome, backache, and other problems.

These radium stones are specially ordered from abroad, and I can provide a small quantity to my patients.

Tamagawa-Onsen: a globally rare hot spring that contains radium

Tamagawa-Onsen is a hot spring located in Senkita city of Akita prefecture. The unique characteristic of this hot spring is that it contains radium called 'Hokutouseki'. This Hokutouseki is almost the same as a radium stone, and is designated as a national treasure.

The radium mineral emanates radium and a very small amount of radioactivity, and it is found only in Tamagawa-Onsen and the Hokutou Hot Springs in Taiwan. The spring contains acidity, carbon dioxide (hydrate), iron, aluminum, and chlorine. It famously has the highest level of acidity among all hot springs in Japan.

Tamagawa-Onsen is also well-known as a hot spring that can cure cancer, a claim that is supported by reports of such cures. This spring is also said to alleviate illnesses such as high blood pressure, arterial stiffening, feminine female ailments, neuralgic pain, skin disease, and asthma.

Geothermal heat exudes from rocky stretches in the hot spring area, making this place also famous for bedrock bathing. Many visitors from throughout Japan come to relax and heal their illnesses here.

Those Who Are Easy to Heal and Those Who Are Not

There are two different types of patients: those who are easy to heal with spiritual healing and those who are not.

In short, those who are easy to heal have the ability to free their minds. These people know very well that they cannot live on their own, and that they are supported by many others and by an invisible power.

To put it another way, healing is successful when the patient can become free of mind. That is the objective of spiritual healing. On the other hand, those who are self-assertive generally do not care about their instinctive roles; they do not thank others and tend to behave egocentrically. They are harder to heal.

Once high levels of energy flow into the body, the patient's original energy will conform to it, and this speeds up recovery. However, if the patient is excessively egotistic, it will take more time for recovery since the two energies will not conform to each other easily.

 Those who cannot be cured by spiritual healing must have given up the possibility of recovering or have reached the natural limit of their lives.

 Although it is almost impossible to know when we are going to die, people with special spiritual talent tend to be able to predict the actual timing. According to the messages I receive from the spiritual world, it seems that the length of all human beings' lives is already decided before they are born. The timing of destined death cannot be postponed even with healing treatment. However, pain can be reduced and death can be accepted comparatively tranquilly. This is in fact much more important than whether the disease is completely cured or not.

 At any rate, the objective of spiritual healing is not to cure those who cannot be cured, but to have the patient realize what the actual cause of the illness was at the level of the soul. Even if the patient was destined to die, fear of death can be dissipated; it is possible to have the patient accept death with a firm determination. It is more important for the patient to realize and accept the true situation. As patients become free of mind and pass away with dignity and tranquility, they can move forward smoothly towards the afterworld. I will explain more on this point later.

 Now I will introduce some cases in order to have you understand about spiritual healing directly in depth.

Healing for Depression and Integrated Disorder Syndrome.

 Mental disorders, including depression and integrated disorder syndrome, are what the methods of spiritual healing can contribute most effectively to in curing patients.

 Both integrated disorder syndrome and depression are caused by spiritual delusions. Those who are caught in depression are obsessed by a depressing spirit, while those who suffer from integrated disorder syndrome are haunted by spirits with the same illness. As the old saying goes, "birds of a feather flock together." Spirits are apt to stay with human beings with a similar energy wave. In order to solve the problem, I must have the patient take my spiritual healing treatment to change the quality of this energy wave, pulling the bad spirit away. It is also important that the patient changes their way of thinking.

 Those who become seriously depressed tend to be too serious, too organized, and have too much curiosity. Among them, a combination of seriousness and uneasiness is the most typical. A person obsessed with perfectionism, feeling that everything must be in order, or that everything must be handled in a certain way, can easily suffer from this type of illness. Too much thinking, which is a result of excess egoism, will not help people become free of mind.

Those who are caught in integrated disorder syndrome tend to be shy and delicate. In most cases, these people are haunted by multiple spirits. They also typically tend to think too much about what's happening, just like those who are in depression.

The biggest problem for those who suffer from depression or integrated disorder syndrome is that they are apt to be concerned about things. Anxiety can be the trigger to any kind of disease.

Even if I have these patients take my treatment, I will not be able to heal them if I cannot change their way of thinking. This is why I give advice tailored to each person, and to their daily condition.

Appropriate Daily Life for Mental Disorder Patients

A cause of mental disorder may be personal character, but another reason may be that the essential energy of the person is too strong or too weak. Anxiety can be brought about when energy is either too strong or too weak. Therefore, it is important to know how to adjust the level of your energy. Though this adjustment can be done through spiritual healing, I also give advice to patients so that they can control their energy level on their own in their daily life.

Recently, many women in their 30s with depression have come to see me. Those who are suffering from serious illness have left their jobs, not even wanting to go outside. They don't feel like doing anything, and decide to just stay in their rooms.

In these comparatively serious cases, most of the time I would ask a patient to take my healing treatment approximately once every seven to ten days. Thus they will be able to maintain a non-depressed condition, which will be maintained for three to five months. If they take my treatment just a few times, they may face a relapse afterwards. Most patients who have recovered to an extent that they could work again are those who tamely followed my advice.

My advice obviously differs between patients, but what is shared with everyone is: "Don't worry too much." I try to keep my advice simple and narrow it down to only one or two points so that they can keep themselves focused.

I always give advice to those who have either too strong or too weak energy. Those with excessive energy tend to keep it inside, not knowing how to release it. In this case, I normally recommend that they practice yoga or other exercises in order to discharge energy. As for those who have a low level of energy, they generally lack sleep and nutrition. In this case, I ask them to change their lifestyle so that they can have a deeper and longer sleep. In order to ensure a better quality of sleep I advise them to undertake certain activities. For example I recommend taking a quiet bath before going to bed, loosening their bodies by practicing yoga, listening to relaxing music, watching healing movies, or reading books.

From a healer's point of view, insomnia, panic syndrome, depression, and integrated disorder syndrome are all brought about by spiritual causes. That is why I give healing treatment and advice to patients of all these illnesses.

Healing Treatment for Alzheimer's and Dementia.

Alzheimer's and dementia, especially most of the juvenile cases of Alzheimer's, come from spiritual causes. However, those who are affected by dementia at the age of 90 or 100 are not influenced by spiritual causes, but by the decline of brain energy that comes from aging.

Moreover, many cases of Alzheimer's are brought about by family problems from a past life. Misunderstandings or disagreements left between two different families in a past life can affect us in our present life. In such case, a member of either family can become ill in order to prevent hatred from remaining. This situation requires a rearrangement of the relationship, such as showing more respect and affection to each other.

We must consider illnesses with a long time span in mind, just like all other events that occur in life. This way of thinking may lighten our burden, for a disease is merely one scene in a dramatic life, which in turn is a precise patchwork of different scenes. Although Alzheimer's is a tragedy for both the patient and other family members, it is a good chance for all of them to seriously face reality and think about the actual causes in order to solve the problem with positive behavior. Seen from such an angle, the reason why a disease occurred can be profoundly understood. That is how severe symptoms of Alzheimer's can be softened.

I have not personally done many healing treatments for those with Alzheimer's but spiritual healing is very effective for patients with this disease, just like other mental disorders that have to do with spiritual causes.

Healing for Atopy, Physical Disability and Voluntary Shut-ins

I put atopy, physical disability, and voluntary shut-ins together because there is a similarity among them. Exactly like Alzheimer's, all of these are illnesses that involve the whole family.

Atopy is found mostly in children, and it has to be solved with the help of the family. Since children cannot go to the hospital themselves, members of the family have to cooperate. The whole family must come together as one and face the disease, which naturally urges the family members to become closer to one another.

Parents and especially children tend to have strong relations from a past life. It is said that parents and children come together in their present lives in order to dissolve the karma that occurred between each other in a past life. Diseases are brought about not just to torment people, but to have people realize the problems that lie between parents and children. If patients can understand the mechanism, they will be able to recover from atopy.

There are quite a few cases in which causes are on the parent's side, not the children's. In these cases, a spiritual disability can be found within the parent. If the parent understands the cause and can improve their mental condition, the child can automatically recover from the illness. In other words, the disease of a child is often taken over from the parent. Therefore, when we face such cases we must look at them from a family point of view. The reason why diseases are often healed as the child grows is either because the problems from the past lives are solved or because the child becomes independent of the parent's influence.

Children who are born with a physical disability are also affected by events in past lives, just like those who have atopy. The reason why a disabled child often torments the parents more than themselves is because the child hopes that the parents notice something important by revealing a problem. In fact there are many cases in which the disabled child lives cheerfully despite the concerns of others. Since physical disability is a serious problem, it can also provide a good chance for the child and the parents to solve problems that have been brought over from past lives.

Voluntary shut-ins can be categorized as a sort of mental disorder. Most of these cases are caused by spiritual factors. Once the child is caught in a shut-in, parents become anxious and concerned. This is another problem that all family members must come together to solve. If the relationship between parents and the child is the core issue the disease can be healed by the parents' efforts, but only after they recognize the actual cause.

These sort of illnesses that involve the whole family can be rapidly solved if the parents become free of mind. Because of this I recommend all family members take my healing treatment together.

Healing Backaches and Knee Aches

Causes of backaches and knee aches differ in each case. Some are caused by spiritual obsession in other parts of the body, such as the internal organs, while others are caused by direct obsessions in the affected area. There are also cases in which mental problems affect the body directly.

Let me introduce an example of a nurse in her forties. She had been suffering from a backache for twenty years. She could not even sleep due to the severe pain that struck her; she couldn't sleep on her back or roll over in her sleep. She had difficulties bending her knees, and she had no choice but to sleep by sitting in a chair with her knees straight.

While directly healing her, I told her that she would be completely healed after three treatments because I sensed this through our conversation. However, she felt that she was already healed when she had a soothing sense in her mind just by listening to my prediction. I held my hand against the affected area for approximately five minutes after that.

It was a week after this when I saw an obvious change in her condition; her pain was reduced, and she could fall asleep lying down in bed. As I continued my healing treatment on her, she became better and better.

In her case, various types of mental stress were causing the backache. That is why I recommended to that she practice exercises for relaxing her back, and to show thanks to the people around her. Just by focusing on her back, she was able to care more about herself. Once she could do that, she would then care more about the people around her as well. This simple change can bring about a great effect.

She also confessed that she never imagined that she could recover using such a method. However, as she kept taking my healing treatments, she was able to easily believe in this approach, which led to a dramatic recovery. In fact, I was able to finish my healing treatments after three sessions, as I had told her at the beginning.

If a patient is strongly influenced by the pattern of daily life, as in this case, it is important to change lifestyles while taking healing treatments. If that is impossible, the patient must focus on refreshing the mind, and make it a habit to take good care of their physical condition.

Healing of Anemia and Backaches.

Let me give you another example of patients recovering from backaches. A. was one of my patients who was suffering from backache that was caused by mental stress. She was a housewife in her 50s, tormented by a serious anemia and backache dating back 30 years. She also had fibroids and a potential stomach cancer, which was found in a physical examination. Her temperature was low and she had stress from caring for her family.

As I held both of my hands against her stomach for eight minutes, she said, "I feel as if something like a hot fireball is soaking into a deep part of my body." In fact she started to sweat heavily on her forehead, which she had to wipe off with her handkerchief after the treatment. After the first healing treatment, she said, "I feel much more comfortable, and it feels as if my body has become lighter." When she came again to take the second treatment, her temperature was higher and her backache was reduced. She told me that her serious pain had disappeared.

I recommended that she listen to relaxing music, appreciate beautiful paintings or other art works, and to have contact with nature. This is because, in most cases, patients can reduce stress and pain just by being free of mind or having contact with a high dimensional energy. If they see that their condition is being improved by spiritual healing, they keep looking for relaxing environments in their daily life.

When she came to see me for the third treatment, she knew that she was already feeling much better, and told me that she had even began to enjoy golf. Her backache was no longer tormenting her like before.

A. wiped her sweat away again after the treatment, but her eyes were shining much brighter than before.

In A.'s case, I was able to fulfill my objective with three consecutive healing treatments and told her that she did not have to come again. It is important for the patients to maintain themselves in good condition after the healing treatment. I tried to imply that keeping a positive mind and grateful attitude is the key to staying healthy.

Thus, after being pushed in the right direction by taking spiritual healing treatment, it is important for the patients to keep a positive mind. Backaches can especially be negatively influenced by stress and anger. Therefore, we must do our best to avoid being emotionally unstable in order to prevent serious symptoms.

Pain on the Right Side of the Body Implies Serious Problems

One time a man in his 40s who had business relations with my clinic came to ask for healing treatment for a pain he had in the back of his shoulder. I did a remote healing for about five minutes that night.

The next day he called me and said, "Did you try healing me around nine o'clock last night?" He told me that he had pain during the day but that it had disappeared around that time. As a matter of fact, that was the time that I did the healing. In his case, one treatment was enough.

His pain was caused by a simple spiritual obsession.

This man had a slight pain on the left side of his body; if patients have pain on the right side, the pain tends to remain for a longer period of time. This is because, in most cases, a person's bad deeds appear as pain on the right side of the body. Although we do not need to care too much about pain on the left side, we must take seriously and think about what we have done if we feel pain on the right side.

In fact, pain on the left side is sometimes a good sign. This is an example whereby negative events occur before positive events in order to adjust the level of energy.

Healing of Diabetes

One day a man in his 60s who had a blood glucose level of 300mg/dl came to my clinic. He was continuously taking medicine provided by a hospital.

I had him take a direct healing treatment with me for about 10 times.

When a patient has a chronic disease, I normally hold my hand against the belly button.

He had average height and weight, but had problems with his diet. Therefore, I asked him to eat more vegetables and control his intake of calories. I also asked him to exercise more often.

It seems that, in many cases, diabetes is caused by the guardian spirit in order to demonstrate that the diet and daily habits of the patient are bad.

If the patient's character is to easily become upset, this can also worsen the illness. It is important to improve the patient's way of thinking at the same time as treatment.

Healing of Hemorrhoids

Many people who have hemorrhoids also come to my clinic. I see that among them there are many egocentric people. If a person is too egocentric, a spirit that conforms to this can cause hemorrhoids. In fact backaches that I have previously discussed can also be caused by strong self-assertiveness. Egocentrism and self-assertiveness mostly come from excessively strong desires.

There was a time when a woman in her late 60s who had had hemorrhoids for over 30 years came to see me. She was very much concerned because she was bleeding almost every day. She had had surgery in the proctology department of a hospital, but in vain.

Three to four days after healing her directly once for five to ten minutes, the bleeding was reduced and completely stopped after ten days. She never showed up after that. Hemorrhoids and hernias are diseases that can be healed very rapidly.

Normally I hold my hand against the patient's stomach when the illness is hemorrhoids. This is because the stomach around the belly button is where energy can be easily absorbed.

Since hemorrhoids are often affected by mental obsessions, changing one's character can naturally cure them. In other words, the patient will suffer from the same symptoms for years if they cannot change the part of their character that makes them easily upset.

Of course, enduring anger all of the time is not recommended. Once you are obsessed with anger you can easily lose control of your emotions. First of all, it is important to accept the fact that you are obsessed and then take actions to remove your concerns.

Healing for Erythromania.

Erythromania is a symptom that involves the face turning red. It can occur when one feels nervous in front of other people. There are many people who suffer from this illness and come to see me to solve their problem. These people often have mental concerns that cause the nervousness and change the flow of blood.

There was a case when a woman in her 40s with this illness came to see me. Improvement could be seen after a few sessions of remote treatment each lasting for five to ten minutes.

There are many possible causes for erythromania, such as changes in hormone levels, but in her case it occurred because her negative feelings came out and caused symptoms when she thought about "ascension." It seems that many recent cases followed the same process as hers.

"Ascension" brings about a change of dimension, which makes people nervous. However, this change does not signify the end of this world or indicate a confused society, as supposed by some people. There is nothing to worry about. Rather, it pushes peoples' minds towards the direction of evolution, which make things better even if natural disasters increase just for the time being. We should always attempt to respond to things positively.

I advised the woman to keep herself relaxed in daily life, since erythromania was a sign of being unnecessarily nervous.

Healing for Insomnia and Excessive Sensitivity to Cold

Patient I.K. was a woman in her fifties who couldn't sleep well from the time she was around forty years old. She took sleeping pills regularly, and when she became fifty years old, she could not find time to relax, as she had to take care of her mother. This situation prevented her from sleeping well even with pills. She tried anything possible, such as acupuncture, chiropractic, and qi, but all in vain.

I began by giving her a remote healing treatment. The first treatment seemed to have given her some tingles, which resembled qi treatment.

The second treatment made her feel warm and gave her a soft and comfortable feeling. She told me that she could maintain the same feeling even after the treatment.

As a result, she became less sensitive to cold than before.

The cause of insomnia is often due to excessive information, which keeps one's nerves overactive. When we get worked up and stressed, it is important to relax our sympathetic nerves and strengthen the parasympathetic nerves instead. However, this has become very difficult in modern times. The more we make an effort to change the situation, the more active our parasympathetic nerves become. Therefore, the best way to handle it is to rely on the effects of spiritual healing.

It is also necessary for those who easily accumulate stress to practice yoga or abdominal respiration, in order to maintain a good physical balance in daily life. Without following these methods, one may develop a serious disease by not having ways to dissipate stress.

Healing for Cancer

Although it depends on each different case, cancer and chronic disease require almost as much time as mental disorder for recovery. Continuous healing is indispensable for curing these illnesses.

Once a patient takes a healing treatment, a good condition is usually maintained for around two weeks, but after that the symptoms tend to come back again.

A few thousand cancer cells are said to be generated per day for a normal person, which means that it is ideal to take treatments every three or four days. A rough target is to take treatments every seven to ten days and repeat this ten times.

Normally, immune cells such as NK cells would destroy cancer cells in order to maintain a healthy condition. However, people who already have symptoms of cancer do not have this mechanism functioning, so it is necessary to restore the normal condition by giving healing treatments and thus reducing the negative energy that generates cancer cells.

Healing for Breast Cancer.

There was the case of a woman in her fifties who had breast cancer and had pain in her sides and ribs. I directly healed her once, and the pain in her ribs on the left side and in the lower part of her left breast dramatically reduced. As the amount of pain declined, her life changed a great deal. She felt relaxed and even food tasted better than before. Spiritual healing can reduce pain in quite a short period of time.

Just for your information, this woman is the one who told me that she could see a person that looked like a local doctor from the Edo era behind me. The next day, after taking the healing treatment, she suddenly woke up in the morning because she was sweating everywhere and exuding a bad smell from her stomach. This seems to be an effect of purification. She was also told by her acupuncture master that her blood vessels were softened.

Since her pain and symptoms disappeared, she insisted on not having surgery later on. However, from a doctor's point of view, I advised her that it was better to remove the affected parts if possible.

She decided to have the surgery after all, and taking remote healing a couple of times before and after it, she recovered smoothly without any pain. She is now living a peaceful life just as she used to before.

Healing for Lung Cancer

A man in his 60s developed lung cancer and came to see me. After I healed him directly, he was free from pain and symptoms. However it was strange to see that the affected area remained according to the radiograph. The only possible interpretation was that the affected area was calcified since cancer cells had ceased their activities.

This man had symptoms such as coughing and difficulty breathing, but he is now living a normal life like before. I had him take seven to eight sessions of five to ten minute direct healing treatments.

Causes of cancer, puzzling diseases and chronic disease are various, but the essential cause normally is the obsession of a filthy spirit. Cancer cells themselves are forms of filthy spiritual energy.

This is why patients with puzzling diseases must change their personality in order to recover health. As I have mentioned many times now, negative thoughts and imagination must be discarded from the level of the soul.

First of all, a refreshment of the mind is required. There are academic conferences that study methods to overcome cancer by laughing. Just laughing from the bottom of the heart and keeping a cheerful and positive mind can heal cancer.

As a matter of fact, taking healing treatments continuously and refreshing your mind can reduce pain and cure serious illnesses, although it may take time.

Causes of Diseases Come From Past Lives

Among those who develop cancer, why do some get stomach cancer while others get breast cancer? Why does the affected area differ from one person to another?

In fact this consequence is strongly influenced by the patient's memory from past lives.

Genes are lumps of memory and information, and contain memories from past lives. The reason why human beings can evolve is because our genes keep memories. We are challenging things in our present life that could not be attained in a past life. We also try to avoid bad incidents in our present life that we experienced in a past life. These actions are taken subconsciously.

According to the message from my guardian spirit, values and appearance also tend to resemble those of ourselves in past lives. My past life is said to be that of Tako Hirose, who was a military man written about in the novel *Saka no ueno Kumo* (Cloud Over the Slope) and my appearance is close to what he looked like.

Diseases found in past lives are also memorized in our genes. If there is a memory of lung problems or lung cancers kept in our DNA, it can remain as a trauma in present life even if the person does not realize it. This may cause certain problems in the lungs for the person in present life.

Hypnotherapy is a method to delete the types of trauma that derive from the past. Fear will be removed by understanding more about what had happened in the past. For example, if there is a person who cannot eat tomatoes due to an incident that happened in a past life, a hypnotherapist will remind the patient of this event in order to remove the fear. This patient will be able to eat tomatoes after taking this therapy. The only thing the hypnotherapist does in this case is clear up a piece of information from the patient's past life.

Although there is a difference in approach, hypnotherapy and spiritual healing are similar in that they both clear up causes of illness. The basic principle of the process is to become free of mind. Waves of free mind can clear up problems. In spiritual healing, we make use of the same methods, regardless of whether the problem is from a past life or the present life.

We cannot cope well with traumatic information that comes from a past life. Since the power of each individual is very small, the only thing that we can truly rely on to protect ourselves from negative energy is the power of others around us.

The Objective of Spiritual Healing

Maurice Barbanell (1902-1981), an Englishman who had the ability to communicate with the spiritual world just like Harry Edwards, discussed spiritual healing with Edwards through a spirit that descended on him called Silver Birch. Birch preaches to people on all aspects of daily life, resembling the assertions of Edwards. However, in this discussion different ideas were exchanged.

Birch says, "Disease is necessary for souls to develop. Therefore, there is no use healing these diseases. It is much more important to accept them ourselves."

Edwards, on the other hand, says, "The objective of spiritual healing is not merely to heal a disease, but to realize what the cause is and to find out whether it can actually be healed or not in the process."

Both points of view hold the objective of development of the soul as a common premise. While Silver Birch insists that healing treatments from others disturb evolution, Harry Edwards says that healing can bring about discoveries that accelerate evolution. They have completely opposite points of view on spiritual healing.

Edwards' conviction is that people can discover facts about themselves that couldn't have been noticed otherwise in the process of healing, such as bad daily habits, bad ways of thinking or feeling, bad attitudes towards family members or others, and wrong ways of showing affection. He insists that this is much more important than solely curing a disease.

I completely agree with this way of thinking, as you might have noticed from what I've tried to explain so far. Disease is not a bad phenomenon in itself. It is merely a phenomenon that presents the negative aspects of an individual. Hence it is more important to realize these problems and drive people in a better direction.

This leads to an evolution of the soul. Diseases and other problems offer opportunities for us to evolve. Once we come to know this, there is no reason for anybody to be concerned. All we have to do is to listen to the voices of our soul, a process in which spiritual healing can help a great deal. Spiritual healing not only has an effect on the physical body, but also can provoke evolution of the soul from a spiritual point of view. This is the greatest advantage of spiritual healing.

Chapter 5
Power Spot Healing

Locations That Hold Extraordinary Energy

The key to spiritual healing is to become free of mind, as I have previously explained and introduced sharing concrete examples of various methods. In this chapter, I will introduce some more simple examples showing how to free your mind. It is called "power spot healing."

Knowledge about power spots came from a rumor among people. It was said that there were locations where special power or energy was radiated, and many people began to explore these places in order to heal themselves or to make their wishes come true. Power spots are known as places where the energy (qi) of the earth is abundant. The rumor was based upon and supported by the concept of "zero magnetic fields."

There are two different types of power spots. One is based on a zero magnetic field that is formed by the uniqueness of the natural environment. The other is based on the existence of spiritual beings.

The former is where magnetic attractions negate each other and consequently create a zero magnetic field. On this planet, the north pole and the south pole both generate geomagnetism. While geomagnetism is generated by a complicated process, resulting in dramatic changes, a zero magnetic field is where there is apparently no magnetism. In reality, geomagnetism is generated here as well, but the powerful fields with opposite directions cancel each other out to create a neutral environment.

One may imagine that nothing is left when you hear the word "zero." However, energy similar to qi is actually generated by a collision of strong geomagnetism in this area. Although it is not yet known how qi is generated, we know that it resembles the energy utilized in spiritual healing. Energy found in a zero magnetic field can be described as immeasurable energy that exists beyond our dimensions.

These genuine power spots such as zero magnetic fields are where we can become free of mind. In other words, if we explore these sites we can expect the same effect as healing treatments.

Sensitive people will either feel the qi or find their mind cleared, and even those who are not sensitive at all can be helped out if they explore a real power spot.

Power spots can also amplify energy and support mental development, just like spiritual healing.

In order to be effectively influenced at a power spot, you must follow the official guidelines that will be explained later. This is a gratuitous method of healing that anybody can adopt, and which I would strongly recommend. I believe it would be a great loss if power spot exploration ends up being of only temporary interest.

Zero Magnetic Fields That Are Generated Where Geomagnetism Collides

Bungui-touge in Nagano prefecture is famous as a place where there is a zero magnetic field. It is located on the median tectonic line, which is the oldest and longest fault formed approximately a hundred million years ago in the area that covers Kanto and Southern-west Japan. On the median tectonic line, there are many shrines, temples and other power spots, such as Kashima-jingu, Suwa-jinja, Ise-jingu, Koya-san, Ken-zan, Ishizuchi-san, and Heitate-jingu.

I can easily understand why people from the past decided to place stone Buddha images and shrines on sites that fall on this median tectonic line because they felt exceptionally strong energy. They regarded these sites as solemn places and took good care of them, which made them special power spots. Another reason for building shrines in this area was possibly to prevent earthquakes from happening, since there are still many active faults on this line.

Although I haven't had the chance to visit all of these places to verify the existence of special energies, it is easy to imagine that there are zero magnetic fields in power spots located on the median tectonic line if we take into account the common relationship of landscape and magnetic fields.

Ise-jingu, Powerful Zero Magnetic Field

The most powerful zero magnetic field that I have ever visited is the Geku of Ise-Jingu. I think it would be quite difficult to find a more powerful one.

Ise-jingu consists of three main parts, the Naigu, the Geku, and the other shrines that surround them. The Naigu is located in the upper reaches of Isuzu River, while the Geku sits in the Yamadagahara field. Most of the tourists mainly visit the Naigu, which enshrines Aamterasu-omikami. Although the official visiting route is to stop by at Geku first and then go on to Naigu, many people limit their visits to the Naigu, since each are as far as six kilometers apart.

I must say that I sensed more power in the Geku rather than the Naigu.

The entire area beyond the front gate is a zero magnetic field radiating powerful energy. When I visited this place, I sensed a soothing feeling and realized that negative qi was being eliminated. It was exactly how I would feel by being healed spiritually.

The healing effect of the Geku is said to be positive for any kind of disease, especially for mental disorders.

Once you finish visiting the Geku, I would recommend spending your time slowly and tranquilly in the neighborhood. The official name of the Geku is Toyouke-taijingu, which implies that it enshrines Toyouke-Omikami, the god protecting food and industry. Since Toyouke-Omikami sits in the Seigu, people tend to move towards home after visiting this single site; however, that is not a wise thing to do.

Actually there are several places that are radiating especially powerful energy in the Geku.

The first unexpectedly powerful location that I must share is Mitsuishi (three stones), which is right by the sacred pond. A solemn rope surrounds a conspicuous arrangement of three round stones. This is said to be where various rituals take place when shrine relocation events take place. In fact you can become purified and free of mind just by standing in that particular place.

In Taganomiya, which is a shrine located on top of a hill named Hinokiyama, the Aramitama of Toyouke-taishingu is enshrined. It can be found after climbing up 98 stone stairs, and this place also radiates a strong qi.

Aramitama represents the aggressive, enterprising and proactive aspect of the two functions of God's soul. The other function represents the calm and tranquil aspect of the soul, which is called Nigimitama. This is enshrined in the Seigu, so I strongly recommend visiting Aramitama, where you will have the chance to walk into this shrine.

At the base of Hinoyama, there is a shrine called Kazenomiya, which is an annex of Ise-jingu. This place is also full of the spiritual energy enshrining Shinatsuhiko-no-mikoto and Shinatobe-no-mikoto. It was originally built to pray for good conditions of wind and rain, which are indispensable for successful agriculture. However, when I visited this place, it began to become windy and the flight I had planned to take from Centrair Airport was cancelled.

I also recommend taking a nice walk in the refreshing woods in the Geku, which has an effect similar to taking a spiritual healing treatment.

Asama-jinja and Spiritual Water at Fujiyoshida

There are many zero magnetic fields in Japan, even in sites that are off the median tectonic line.

The officially called Kitaguchi-hongu Fuji Asama-jinja is one of them. The main goddess enshrined here is Kohnohanasakuyahime-no-mikoto, who lets people sense different types of energy.

There are cedar trees on both sides of the approach to the shrine. In these types of places, where qi is flowing properly, plants grow lively and steadfastly. The reason why the sacred trees are great in size is not only because they are exposed to people's prayers, but also because the shrines are built in locations with good qi. Sites where plants grow well even if there aren't any shrines can be called power spots.

I felt especially strong energy when I stood in front of the Fujitaro-sugi, which is said to be the most sacred tree in Fujiasama-jinja. My hands started to tingle just by standing in front of the tree. After ten minutes, I felt as if I had been transported to a different world in another dimension.

Fujiasama-jinja is also known for the spiritual power of its divine water. The fountain on the left-hand side of the main shrine is mainly used by visitors to purify their hands, but people from remote places also come to take the water back home. This water is derived from a natural spring, which is located three kilometers away from the shrine. It is the sacred water of Mount Fuji.

Power spots, in fact, tend to be located where water is pure and clean. We have many power spots in Japan because there is an abundant underground water supply in this country. Bearing this in mind, the quantity of special power in Japan has started to decline, however, due to illegal dumping of industrial waste, the utilization of pesticides, and chemical substances released from factories and households that contaminate the water.

Shiraito Waterfall with Zero Magnetic Field and Minus Ion Relaxation Effects

The Shiraito waterfall, known as a summer retreat in Karuizawa Nanago, is also a wonderful zero magnetic field. Here the water is clean and pure, contributing to the fresh atmosphere in this specific area.

By visiting this place, we can have our body and soul purified of negative qi. Moreover, those who are tired or have excessive energy can refresh themselves by taking in fresh air full of minus ions. They may expect the same sort of effect as spiritual healing.

Meiji-jingu is Full of Spiritual qi

Meiji-jingu is a special place where a zero magnetic field that is created by natural energy is also combined with spiritual energy.

The Meiji Emperor and Empress Shoken are enshrined here.

Powerful qi can be sensed here, and I personally have experienced strange incidents such as seeing the doors and windows of a car open by themselves. When this happened I felt a certain energy that made me believe that the Meiji Emperor used to have special spiritual talents.

I felt the most powerful energy from the forest on the right-hand side after passing the Torii gate. By walking through this area, you will be able to refill yourself with positive energy.

The forest in Meiji-jingu is artificial. It consists of 100,000 trees of 365 different species that were delivered from all around the country, and required the mass cooperation of 110,000 volunteers to establish.

Yoyogi was chosen as the location for this shrine following the lyrics of the theme song for the Meiji Emperor.

Districts that were prosperous even after the Great Kanto Earthquake or the Great Tokyo Air Raids are often protected by spiritual energy. Among these places, the Meiji-jingu is said to be protected by the most powerful and special spiritual energy, which is the imperial family itself.

Because the imperial family has ruled for a long period of time I feel spiritual energy from the presence of this family. Authority and reins of power that persist for a long time are usually protected by spirits. The family emblem of the imperial family is made up of the 16 flower petals of a chrysanthemum, and this number "16" is also said to have a special power. Another important point to mention is that the traditional rituals of the imperial family are designed to bring about connections with spiritual power. Also, the family apparently has sufficient energy to support the birth of psychics and those with special spiritual talents, examples of which are found in the birth of the Meiji Emperor and the Showa Emperor.

Another example of a long-lasting ancestry that is supported spiritually is the British royal family. They possess vast land around the world and still have spiritual power over the people as head of the Anglican church. However, we can say that they were even more powerful during the time when they were at the height of their prosperity. They were most powerful when Harry Edwards was alive. We can imagine that the royal family and Harry Edwards attracted each other, playing a special role together in influencing people spiritually.

The Attractive Nyorai Power of Zenko-ji.

Zenko-ji in Nagano prefecture is a power spot defined by spiritual power.

Although I cannot sense a soothing feeling that clears my mind, as in Ise-Jingu, I do feel a sensory protection in this temple. If people who are suffering a disease were to visit this place, they would be welcomed by a healing energy. If those with strong wishes were to visit, they would be automatically supported and have their wishes come true. This is due to the power of Amidanyorai, which has always demonstrated an edifying will towards all human beings.

In Zenko-ji, there is an active power that continuously attracts people. After it was founded 1400 years ago, all of those who were in power at the time visited this temple without fail. As many as six million people visit Zenko-ji every year, especially during the years of Gokaicho (when there are open exhibition of special parts of the temple). This occurs once every seven years, and seven million people covering five percent of the total population of Japan visit this place at this time. The Dalai Lama also visited Zenko-ji last year.

I personally did not intend visiting Zenko-ji, but I was given the chance two years ago when I was asked to appear in a live TV program. I felt that I was led by some sort of power at that time, and since then I've made it a routine to visit there every month. I believe Zenko-ji has the same type of attractive power as the Ebisu god among the seven gods of good fortune. The source of this power can be found in the main temple of Zenkjo-ji.

In the main temple, the statue of ikko-sanzon-amidanyorai, which is said to be the oldest Buddha image in Japan, is enshrined. It was brought to Japan in the sixth century from Kudara (a country that existed in the Korean Peninsula) together with Buddhism.

I have already explained about Amidanyoura in Chapter 3. If you do visit this place, you will be able to confirm that divine power is brought down to earth.

Within the confines of Zenko-ji, I felt the strongest energy on the left-hand side of the hall of worship. The energy of Amidanyorai is similar to that of Tenkai, and I thought it was completely different from what would directly benefit us in living in modern society.

If you wanted to pursue actual benefits in this world, you should visit Takeda-jinja in Kofu, Yamanashi. They say that Shingen Takeda, who was a famous warlord, was never defeated because he always prayed at this shrine before heading to the battlefield. It is also well-known as a shrine that brings about success in commercial activities.

The energy of Amidanyorai is so extraordinary that it seems to originate from a different dimension; it is even special among other types of Buddhas. The great Buddha in Kamakura is also an Amida-type Buddha, attracting many people with that tremendous energy.

Amidanyorai is said to be most influential to human lives; it is a presence that wishes to support people naturally. The energy of Amidanyorai will become more and more important in an era of dramatic change.

Kannon and Bosatsu, on the other hand, are energies that are closer to human beings; they are more like guardian spirits.

Locations That Are Purified by qi from the Ocean

Rituals of purification are carried out where there is a waterfall or a river, or where there was an ocean long ago. Water innately has the power to purify things. In oceans, this function is strengthened because it comes together with salt, which also has purifying energy. At the same time oceans also provide energy to enrich natural vital power.

Among shrines that are said to be power spots utilizing the qi of oceans, I would introduce the coast of Kamakura, which in my personal experience I have found to be especially powerful.

The vicinity of the coast in Kamakura, particularly the area covering the Koshigoe seacoast to Shichirigahama, is an area where marine energy and magnetic energy meet. Therefore it is said to have extraordinary power.

Tsurugaoka-hachimangu and the Great Buddha of Kamakura are locations of especially high energy, so you would have a pleasant time just by walking around the neighborhood after visiting these power spots.

As is widely known, meditating while walking is a good way to clear your mind.

The Best Way to Make Use of Power Spots

You do not have to make a wish or to pray at power spots. You will benefit just by spending time there. However, there is some preparation that can make your stay much more effective.

First of all, you must not take negative emotions with you. This is because sometimes negative emotions can be amplified in these places.

If you do visit a shrine, wash your hands and mouth with the purifying water, and clear your mind as well. You should be thankful for everything and follow the order of two bows and two claps; monetary offerings are another way to show your gratitude.

You must maintain the same feelings and attitudes when you visit a temple. It is important to put your hands together in prayer with tranquil and modest thoughts in mind.

The more powerful the locations you visit are, the more negative or more positive the consequences become. Thus you should remember to keep in mind the correct procedures to follow on visiting.

If you can visit power spots several times a year on a regular basis, you will have better luck. Although it does not matter too much where you visit, it is always better to visit the same shrine or other power spots that you are fond of. This is because places that you are familiar with provide a special atmosphere that can relax you.

At these power spots you become free of mind by making contact with special energy, which makes it easier for you to connect with your guardian spirit. It is not God but the guardian spirits that can actually help you realize your hopes.

In other words, power spots are where you can express your thanks and awe towards the guardian spirits and heaven. It is also where you can experience an extraordinary version of yourself with an ultimately pure mind.

In power spot healing, it is most important to relinquish your concerns and to acquire a refreshing and solemn attitude.

If you can't visit these places for some reason, you should find time to thank God and Buddha by recalling how you felt on visiting shrines in the past.

How to find places where you can become truly happy

You will be able to lead a happy life in good health if you always remember to do your best to change negative energy to positive energy.

It is also important to carefully choose where to live. In the olden days, authorities designed their mansions by making use of Fusui principles. Buildings that have survived a long time are always protected by Fusui or spiritual energy. Meiji-jingu is one of them, and the Imperial Palace, Nikko Toshogu, and Sensou-ji are also in the same category.

If you are willing to look for a place to live, you should remember to choose somewhere with clean water, good wind, and plants that grow well. Places that have the characters "dai" (hill) or "yama" (mountain) would also be a good option.

Locations with clean water usually have high levels of waves. Fujiyoshida in Yamanashi is said to be a city with the lowest water costs in Japan, and this is due to the fact that they can use the abundant spring water of Mt. Fuji.

Tokyo has clean water for a large city. There are two main reasons for Tokyo being one of the most energetic cities in the world. One is because it has abundant water, and the other is because it has the advantage of its Fusui location. New York in the United States is also known as a city of abundant water and has become a prosperous city because there are many forests that can hold many water sources.

Japan used to be full of good qi as a country, since it was gifted with good forests as well as much water. However, due to the contamination of rivers by pesticides and the interruption of water flow caused by excessive dam construction, the energy level is on a decline. It is sad to see this happening in our country.

Choosing Power Spots by Their Names

It is also useful to choose where to live by names.

For example, 'Aobadai' and 'Daikanyama' are said to be good names because they have characters that mean "hill" or "mountain." These places are located on hills as expressed in their names, and therefore they tend to have fine winds passing by, which bring about positive energy. On the contrary, names that have 'Tani' in them, which means "valley" in Japanese, are located in a low areas where wind cannot pass through; therefore, negative qi will remain in the same places. You would be advised to avoid choosing these places.

The area that I personally feel high levels of energy from these days is from Yamate Street in Daikanyama to Aobadai. In the Hill Side Terrace in Daikanyama there is an ancient burial mound called Sarugakuduka. It is obvious that this place has strong energy from long ago, and I recommend this place for a weekend walk since you can refresh yourself just by walking around this area. The view from Saigoyama Park also offers you an extraordinary experience, which is much more than one can normally expect in Tokyo.

It is said that there are many people with spiritual talent living in the area that covers Meiji-jingu and Omotesando. I believe these types of people are attracted to this area because Meiji-jingu is a special place where we can connect with the spiritual world. They can be more effective doing their jobs at this place due to the exceptional convenience.

A Method for Changing Your Home Into a Power Spot

It is important to keep your homes comfortable in order to maintain the level of your luck and health.

Methods of changing your home into a power spot differ according to where you live and who you are. For this reason, it is better for you to consult an expert on Fusui for particular details. However, I believe it is helpful to introduce a method that anybody can try.

In your home, the most important places are those that have to do with water, such as toilets and bathrooms. As I mentioned in Chapter 2, putting these facilities in good locations is not recommended because good luck will be consumed. Instead it is important to keep these in bad locations instead.

Moreover, places with water are where you can connect well with Yukai; you must always keep them clean to prevent trapping negative energy inside your homes. It is also important to keep the doors of bathrooms and the tops of toilets closed.

The next place of priority is the bedroom. Since it is the place where you spend at least one-third to one-fourth of your life, you must arrange it so that you can always have a relaxing rest.

Bedrooms should be located in places that can comfort you best. However, you must avoid placing them next to the toilet. If you put the bedroom near the toilet you can be caught by bad spirits quite easily.

Arranging the bed so that your head does not face doors, windows, or mirrors is also recommended. If you do so, you will be directly exposed to the flow of qi, which will prevent you from experiencing a deep and comfortable sleep.

It is also important to arrange your rooms so that you can absorb as much sunshine in the morning as possible. I will not go into further details on this point since it all depends on where you choose to live.

Another effective way is to bring in qi of plants. Plants can absorb bad qi and protect us. I believe you may have experienced plants dying when something bad occurred to you or when somebody around you passed away. This happens because plants absorb the negative energy that is influencing you. The condition of the plants around you can tell us a lot about the environment you live in.

Plants are also inhabited by spirits. We decorate household altars with certain plants because they are more easily inhabited by spiritual presences than metallic substances. Sometimes when we cut down trees suddenly, without notice, spirits can be surprised and generate negative energy that influences human beings and other animals. If we need to cut trees down, we must remember to conduct rituals to apologize beforehand.

Above all, the positive mind of those who are living at home is most important.

It is said that people of the Inca Empire lived happily and calmly for several hundred years just by praying to God and without using any advanced technology, such as flood-control construction. However, they perished eventually because they reduced the amount of praying and spent more time and energy on building dams and other facilities.

Ancient civilizations used to be prosperous because the people showed pure and modest attitudes when praying to God. Once they lost that virtue, they were doomed to perish and this was followed by a steady decline of their energy. I believe this is a significant warning for us if we want to lead our civilization towards a glorious future.

Chapter 6
To Be Healed From the Soul in the Era of Ascension

The Entire Planet Earth Will Become a Power Spot in 2012

Have you ever heard of the word "ascension"? Ascension refers to the rise of dimensions. In 2012 the materialistic three-dimensional world that we are living in will move on to a higher level of spiritual dimension.

Many spiritual leaders have discussed this ascension. Some of them insist that it is connected with the doomsday theory. This is based on the Maya calendar, which ends in December of 2012. They believe that human beings will perish at this time and, although there is little chance of this happening, many incidents suggest that the likelihood is actually increasing.

Ascension will increase its speed as we approach 2012 and it is said that many people will experience an awakening at this time. An awakening of the soul can change you into a higher dimensional form of energy. Sri Bhagavan, who is an Indian clergyman, asserts that 70,000 people will experience an awakening at the end of 2011. This man is one of the leaders of the spiritual world, who influences many celebrities and intellectuals in Japan.

Why will such a phenomenon occur? The answer to this question can only be explained as follows: the universe was made to bring this ascension about and a sacred entity that created this universe must have planned the event in the first place.

In this ascension, the entire solar system will be transformed into a higher dimension. This type of ascension has happened in the past. However, it is difficult for us to recognize because it only happens approximately once in 10 billion years.

The magnetic field of the earth becomes zero once every 30 billion years, and this will happen in the year 2012. When this event occurs, the entire planet will become a zero magnetic field.

Some reports have already been announced about the weakening of the earth's geomagnetism and the movement of the North and South Pole. I assume that these symptoms are seen because the earth is waiting to become a zero magnetic field in 2012.

As I have explained in the previous chapter, zero magnetic fields are sites that generate powerful qi and energy, which often cure people's diseases or make their wishes come true. Therefore, ascension will essentially change the earth into one great power spot.

Such a precious chance that only arrives once every 30 billion years will occur shortly.

Ascension Changes the World

How will our lives and ourselves be affected by this ascension?

As there are some people who can't sense the energy when visiting power spots, there may therefore be people who don't notice that it happened. However, it is not important whether you notice or not. The influence is already approaching each one of us, and there are concrete changes happening all around us.

First of all, human values will shift from material to spiritual issues. In real life, the value of money itself will decline.

Another possible shift is a greater focus on the inside rather than the outside, meaning that people will give priority to spiritual satisfaction. In Japan, a movement called 'Danjari' is becoming increasingly popular. This movement promotes a change of lifestyle by redefining the relationship between products and human beings. Material values should be subsumed by a more human spiritual value, which may be an effective approach to enriching our lives.

Nowadays there are many additional opportunities to look deeply into ourselves, apart from these proactive movements. For example, diseases and injuries, changes of profession, loss of jobs, and troubles caused among friends or family members actually occur to provide chances to recognize important principles.

If you do not recognize many of these principles, troubles may frequently occur around you. These troubles are provided so that you can learn and overcome them in order to experience an awakening of the soul. Thus the universe encourages people on earth, regardless of their nationality; this is a significant process that is accompanied by ascension.

For example, if you face a situation where you must change your job, this becomes a necessity, whether positive or negative. What is more important is whether you have a passion for and motivation towards your job. You must not compare the amount of time you spent in the job with the amount of money that you earn; instead you must seriously consider whether the job is beneficial to yourself and society over time. This new perspective is becoming more and more important.

Many of you may already have learned to focus on fulfilling your god-given role by working hard in your particular field.

After ascension, hidden truths will be revealed and disingenuous people will be eliminated. It will be much easier to understand how others feel, further facilitating communication without words. It will be more difficult to hide misdeeds.

Convulsion of Nature That Will Occur After Ascension

The theory insisting that human beings will perish in 2012 equates to expecting convulsions of nature such as earthquakes, serious floods or other disasters. The North Pole may switch places with the South Pole, submerging continents and bringing about tsunamis. Thus the earth will experience a dramatic change, which will eliminate many lives. There are in fact many phenomena already happening around the world that can be associated with ascension.

Some experts say that the mass death of honey bees, fishes, and birds reported all over the world are forerunners of polar migration. Birds, for example, are said to fly by sensing geomagnetism, so it is easy to imagine that they could lose their way if the earth's magnetism changes.

Global warming is one of the events that have already started to occur because of ascension. Although it is said that the temperature of the earth is rising due to mass emissions of carbon dioxide, which is a consequence of daily human activities, the truth is that the rise of temperature is bringing about the increase of carbon dioxide.

In fact there are some scientists who support this theory. The origin of global warming theory was identified by Mr. Keeling, who reported research that demonstrated the relationship between the amount of carbon dioxide in the atmosphere and the temperature of the earth. It was originally reported that the temperature rose after an increase of carbon dioxide, but later it was said to be the opposite: that the amount of carbon dioxide increased after an increase in the temperature. However, since the former result was reported first, other scientists came to support it.

Even scientists who insist that a rise of temperature occurs first do not know why this actually happens. For an unknown reason, the temperature of the earth rises and brings about an increase of carbon dioxide in the air.

As I explained earlier, ascension is accompanied by a rise of temperature and there is a possibility that many other convulsions of nature are associated with ascension as well. Changes that we already see around the world are also signs that the earth is preparing for a shift to a new dimension.

However, I do not believe that such a change will result in the destruction of human civilization. Although great damage may result, it is more important not to fear such change and instead accept it as a process for the realization of significant principles and as an opportunity to improve your spiritual abilities. This attitude will surely be more beneficial to both you and society.

Ascension May Cause a Crisis That Leads to the End of Mankind

When we say global warming is not caused by an increase of carbon dioxide in the atmosphere, some may believe this means that eco-friendly actions are not necessary; however, this is a grave misunderstanding.

The best eco-friendly action to take is not to decrease carbon dioxide emissions, but to avoid further pollution of the earth.

Even though the increase of carbon dioxide production after the industrial revolutions of the 19th and 20th centuries is perceived as the main problem, we must keep in mind that the expansion of chemical substances is causing more serious problems globally.

There are many theories accounting for why honey bees are dying off or disappearing in mass quantities. They include changes in geomagnetism, changes in genes, the effects of viruses, and the effects of chemical pesticides. I personally believe that artificial causes such as the changes of genes and the effect of chemical pesticides are especially influential.

A new type of chemical pesticide called Neonicotinoid is said to be influencing honey bees. The range of effect for a phospho-organic pesticide used to be only several hundred meters, whereas Neonicotinoid may spread to a range of four kilometers. It can cause an increased negative effect on honey bees of up to 400 times compared to the traditional pesticide. It is also said that human nerves can also be gravely affected.

This pesticide is banned in the EU because it is too harmful to animals. In Japan, it has been legally accepted after setting a stricter criteria for its use.

There is also another type of pesticide called Clothianidin that is related to Neonicotinoid, used mainly for growing tea. The accepted amount of Clothianidin is set at 50ppm for tea, 15ppm for Chinese leeks, and 1-5ppm for celery, tomatoes, green peppers, cucumbers, mandarin oranges, and pears. These amounts are much higher than the 0.01ppm that has been set by the positive list system.

There are approximately 20 million species of animals on earth. Of these, 50,000 to 150,000 are said to be becoming extinct (100-300 a day) every year. Tropical rainforests full of wild animals are especially facing a serious situation whereby species are becoming extinct 10,000 times faster than the natural pace. The World Bank also reports that 25% of plants and birds in tropical rainforests will become extinct within 30 years. Normally, where the ecological system is stable, there are a wide variety of species. However, if there is a clear sign of a reduction in diversity, it must mean that the ecological system is being destroyed, and this can easily be associated with the crisis of mankind.

If ascension does not occur smoothly because of the contamination of the earth, more adjustment will be required, which may cause the convulsion of the natural situation to deteriorate.

The most important rule that we must follow now is not only to reduce carbon dioxide emissions but to avoid contaminating our planet. Moreover, we must keep our bodies and souls clean, and continue acting with a pure heart.

Some people use the term "clean energy," but we must be careful about judging how clean certain energy really is. Electric cars are said to be clean because they do not produce gas emissions. However, if the electric energy does not originate from natural energy sources (nuclear power is not included), it is not eco-friendly. It is important for us to think about what claims are true and which are false, making sure our values are not easily influenced by the mass media.

Natural disasters will always increase and cannot be stopped, even by the self-purifying effect of the earth. However if we can shift our mental abilities towards a higher dimension during the process of approaching a zero magnetic field, there is hope for avoiding a disastrous situation.

Yukai Will Ascend Along with Ascension

Many negative phenomena will also occur along with ascension.

As the dimension is changing with the onset of ascension, the dimension of Yukai is also experiencing a critical change. It is so serious that Yukai itself may disappear after 2012. If this happens, spirits that have energy such as envy or resentment will lose their place and begin to approach human beings.

In other words it will become easy for people with negative waves to develop diseases such as depression or mental disorder. We must be careful to avoid this.

Yukai does not have an actual form. It was originally created by delusions caused by human emotions. When we approach a zero magnetic field, things that do not exist in reality will disappear. Negative energy that will lose the reason to exist is currently making a great flutter before it comes to an end.

Since negative energy will invite other types of energy of the same kind, it is important to control your body and soul so that you don't store emotions such as envy or resentment. Spiritual healing can be effective in supporting you with this task, especially in such a critical period of time.

The death penalty is not a good method of punishment because those who are executed can obsess over others and make them commit crimes of the same kind. It is better to clean the perpetrators' souls rather than to simply kill them. I would also recommend taking spiritual healing treatments for this purpose.

Zero Magnetic Fields Facilitate Connections with the Tenkai

I have already explained that people can easily connect with guardian spirits in a zero magnetic field because one can become mind-free with less effort. Now I must also point out that as the earth itself becomes a zero magnetic field by ascension, connection with Tenkai, a higher level of energy, will also be facilitated.

This can be explained with the following analogy; people become more exposed to the power of the sun due to the clearance of clouds that had been in the way.

In the same way, the inspiration and sensitivity of people will be enriched.

As I have mentioned previously, we may be able to understand things that we could not beforehand, be able to intuit what people have in mind without directly communicating, or understand others' personalities more easily than before. Some people may even be reminded of their past lives; others may be realize a special talent, such as X-ray vision, etc.

Seemingly ridiculous things may become common sense, and vice versa.

During such a period of time, there is no reason to follow the conventional rules or habits; it is more important to prioritize what seems important for you. In order to judge what is valuable or important, you must not think directly but instead try to feel with your heart. If you can connect with a higher level of energy, this will become possible. If you are able to judge things quickly and correctly, you will be able to lead a fruitful life both privately and professionally.

I previously mentioned that Sri Bhagavan said that 70,000 people will experience an awakening. Awakening reduces the difference between a higher level of energy and your own energy level, which means that many people will be able to acquire a higher dimensional energy.

Our Future Will Be Supported by Spiritual Healing

Once you reach a certain level, you will be able to avoid developing diseases since potential causes will be eliminated.

An ideal society without police or doctors may not be an unreachable dream.

The objective of spiritual healing is also to reconsider the core source of various problems and bring about the awakening of the soul necessary for creating an appropriate order in society.

Harry Edwards writes in his book as follows: "I am witnessing God's plan to influence our lives by conducting new activities of spiritual healing." The meaning of "God's plan" is also explained by him: "The great objective to eliminate war, poverty, greed, and any other abject concepts by broadening people's views and purifying people's way of living through spiritual healing." What he has in mind is "the well-ordered intentional evolution of human beings."

Ascension occurs because the energy that can be called "God's plan" exists in the program of the universe. Spiritual healing is also contributing a great deal in the evolution of our soul in this process.

If we can become mind-free and abandon egoism through spiritual healing, the quantity of disease and many problems will dramatically decrease, enabling us to understand the true value of happiness. During the period of ascension, we may be able to make this a global event.

Moreover, an awakening of the soul frees us from the fear of death. We will understand that the death of the body is not an end, and that it is merely a staging point in the evolution of the soul. If this is completely understood, death would not involve as much sadness and we would be able to move on more smoothly and with less trauma and suffering.

Spiritual healing is not a mere remedy. It is certain that spiritual healing will become a powerful driving force behind people's awakening.

Spiritual healing is necessary and relied upon by many people, especially in this time of ascension. If more and more people come to experience an awakening of the soul, a better environment will be created for others to experience the same thing. The speed of global ascension will increase and, if the change of dimension is smoothly attained, a whole new world that can make everyone's wishes come true will arrive.

Spiritual healing is a method to support the ascension of each one of us, and as a result it will contribute to the future establishment of an orderly earth, one that perfectly conforms to the program of the universe.